THE MAKING OF A
CHEF

LUKE MANGAN

NH
NEW HOLLAND

Published in 2010 by
New Holland Publishers (Australia) Pty Ltd
Sydney • Auckland • London • Cape Town

www.newholland.com.au

1/66 Gibbes Street Chatswood NSW 2067 Australia
218 Lake Road Northcote Auckland New Zealand
86 Edgware Road London W2 2EA United Kingdom
80 McKenzie Street Cape Town 8001 South Africa

Copyright © 2010 in text: Luke Mangan
Copyright © 2010 in images: Luke Mangan, unless otherwise indicated.
Copyright © 2010 cover photograph: Adrian Lander
Copyright © 2010 New Holland Publishers (Australia) Pty Ltd

All rights reserved. No part of this publication may be reproduced, stored in a retrieval system or transmitted, in any form or by any means, electronic, mechanical, photocopying, recording or otherwise, without the prior written permission of the publishers and copyright holders.

National Library of Australia Cataloguing-in-Publication Data:

Mangan, Luke.

The making of a chef / Luke Mangan, Anthony Huckstep.

ISBN: 9781741108156 (pbk.)

1. Mangan, Luke.
2. Cooks--Australia--Biography.
3. Cooking.

641.5092

Publisher: Diane Jardine
Publishing manager: Lliane Clarke
Project editor: Talina McKenzie
Written by Anthony Huckstep
Proofreader: Catherine Etteridge
Designer: Donnah Dee Luttrell
Cover photograph: Adrian Lander
Production manager: Olga Dementiev
Printer: Ligare Book Printers, Sydney, New South Wales

FOREWORD

As I put the finishing touches on this book, I consider myself to be one of the luckiest guys around. I guess you'll see that once you've read this book, but you will also see that it wasn't delivered on a silver platter and nor did I expect it to be.

For more than half my life I've been surrounded by food and restaurants. I love it so much I could never imagine doing anything else. The business is full of challenges, as is any I guess, and as our industry struggles to develop chefs and retain them, I worry what will happen in the future. I hope that my story helps inspire some of the young chefs coming through to stick at it.

This is my story: the ups and the downs, the challenges, the passion, and the commitment required to make it.

I truly believe if someone wants something bad enough, they will get it. So this is for any young chef who is thinking of throwing it in because the hours are too long, the money isn't enough and your head chef is tough on you. There is a light at the end of the tunnel, there is a future in this wonderful world of restaurants and yes there will be people ready to knock you down, but my only advice is, don't ever quit!

Enjoy my story.

- Luke Mangan

'Luke Mangan is the Michael Corleone of Sydney. A colossus. Don't go drinking with him. Last time I hung with him, I crawled home like a whipped dog.'
Anthony Bourdain

CONTENTS

PART ONE

1	Check Chef	9
2	Family Feast	15
3	Mingy and the Misfits	21
4	Done Deal, But the Devil's in the Detail	32
5	Finding My Feet, But Landing on My Head	39
6	Sanctity of the Seaside	45
7	Tragedy Strikes	51
8	The Phone Call	56
9	The Waterside Inn	62
10	KP and Rowley Leigh	70
11	Bread and Wine	79
12	Rowley Gets Snookered, and I Get Bowled Over	86

PART TWO

13	Rogues to Riches	97
14	The Big Break	104
15	Class Of '95	111
	Recipes	*120*

16	Cards Dealt to Single Diners	123
17	Turning Sausages into Salt	131
18	Striking Gold in the Salt Mines	137
19	The Empire Expands	145
20	All Within My Hands	151
21	In Bed With Virgin	156
22	Dealt A Royal Flush	166
	Recipes	*170*
23	Young Blood	172

PART THREE

24	Dreams Dashed, But Tokyo Promises	185
25	Home Base	192
26	US on Radar, But Venture Heads South	201
27	Getting My Sea Legs	208
28	These Days	213

| Acknowledgements | 223 |

PART ONE

*'Regrets, I've had a few...
But then again, too few to mention.'*

Frank Sinatra

1

CHECK CHEF

I'm not the best chef in the world. Hell, some would argue that I'm not even the best chef on my street. And that's totally fine. The truth is, there was every chance I wasn't going to be a chef at all. But, like most people I guess, there were defining moments in my life when I realised just who I was and what I was capable of.

For much of my apprenticeship I hated it. Half the time it felt like all I was doing was washing dishes, peeling potatoes or shelling peas like I was being punished for letting the team down. It was like being in the army. Yes chef, no chef, three bags full chef. There was no letting up of the wave of verbal barrages barked my way and the long hours really took their toll on me. These days you certainly couldn't get away with the sort of discipline handed out back then—the verbals, a little push into line, a kick up the bum and even pots thrown across the room (although never directed at anyone, and certainly no one was physically abused). It was just a tough environment. It was really something I had never experienced, and for a 15-year-old kid from a middle class family it was quite confronting. I guess in truth I never really felt like a chef during my apprenticeship. Sure, I'd found something I could finally sink my teeth into, but it was a hard grind, especially for a teenager.

I was lucky enough to do my apprenticeship under one of Australia's finest chefs of the 1970s and '80s, Hermann Schneider. His restaurant Two Faces was one of the best, if not *the* best, in the country. Over the four years of my apprenticeship I bounced between three of Schneider's venues: Two Faces, Roesti Bistro and, in the later years, Delgany Country House Hotel in the southern seaside town of Portsea, Victoria.

If you think Gordon Ramsay is tough in the kitchen, well Gordon's a puppy dog compared to Hermann Schneider. Looking back now, I am glad he was like that. It made me the chef I am, and set the standard for how a top kitchen should run.

Every day around midday, Hermann used to come in from the markets. One day he walked straight into the downstairs kitchen at Roesti Bistro where I was cooking. I had my first order of deep-fried whiting in the fryer. Hermann took one look at it and said, 'The fish is done Luke, take it out.'

I replied, 'No, no I just put it in, Mr Schneider, it's not done yet.'

'Look at the fucking fish, it's fucking cooked Luke, when I say it's cooked, it's cooked!'

Hermann pulled the fish out of the basket with his tongs, burning his hand in the process, and put the fish on the rack. He was right, the fish was cooked. I realised then never to question him again.

The reality of those days was: either toughen the hell up and fall into line with his system or pick another trade. The working week wasn't 40 hours and nine to five, it was 70 plus hours and usually 7am until midnight. Hermann was a hard taskmaster. I guess his right-hand man and head chef, John Lepp, acted as a buffer between Hermann and all the chefs. John was the meat in the sandwich in some ways. I think he thought that if you have good kids, you have to look after them and nurture them. It was almost good cop, bad cop. Hermann dealt with things differently, but they both had the same goal. If a chef didn't work hard and wasn't a good person then they were pushed out.

Hermann didn't see cheffing as artistic and glamorous as it is perceived to be these days. Chefs weren't celebrities; chefs were tradesmen. He believed that if you could cook for 200 people and satisfy them in a night, it didn't mean you were a genius. It simply meant you did your job.

Both Hermann and John really wanted someone who could grind it out when the shit hit the fan in a commercial kitchen. There's no doubt that talent had a role to play, but it was a bit of a trade by attrition in those days. It had a big impact on me.

I have to be honest though, I was probably the worst apprentice anyone could have. I didn't think. I didn't remember, I had no common sense and I had the attention span of a gnat. I still do. I recently caught up with Hermann and he happily reminded me that he had apprentices who had more flair than me and were much more focused too, but I worked very hard, which was nice to hear, I think.

I went home in tears many times. Discipline and commitment isn't a trait you are born with, it's something you learn. My dad was the first to drill that into me. Work hard and then work harder the next day, and so on. It's about respect for yourself. There were many occasions that I wanted to throw in the towel, but for some reason I didn't.

CHECK CHEF

Hermann was a tough bugger, but I can totally understand the man. He could seem completely irrational at times, but once you understood what he was trying to achieve, it made sense. As a young kid doing your apprenticeship you don't realise that this is one man's business. His life. His reputation. Every morsel that leaves the kitchen puts his reputation on the line and could mean the difference between a restaurant that closes its doors and one that flourishes every service. If I put that in jeopardy, then I deserved a bollocking.

Once you understood that—and he drilled it into you, let me tell you—you soon realised that when he's yelling at you in service it doesn't really matter. It's not personal. His objective was to get the best out of you, and deliver the best possible outcome for the guest. It was never, ever personal. If you couldn't cut the mustard and maintain that standard, then you knew where the door was. You just need to concentrate on delivering a good product. It's simple: you deliver a good consistent product then you don't get a bollocking.

Hermann used to tell me, 'I expect an enormous amount from anyone who works in my kitchen. I have the same respect for someone who is a good kitchen hand and a chef who does his job properly. I don't care what role you have, as long as you do your job properly.'

One service at Delgany, towards the end of my apprenticeship, changed my life forever.

Although I had worked under his watchful eye for a few years already, I had yet to step up to the plate and cook on the meat/sauce section... next to Hermann Schneider. But that night had finally arrived. I was almost qualified as a chef, but I was still far from being a real chef. It was a Saturday night, the restaurant was fully booked and this was either going to be the best day of my life and make me, or he'd rip me to shreds and break me.

LUKE MANGAN

The orders started coming in and I just put my head down and shut the whole world out. For the entire evening I was sweating bullets and internally I was probably second-guessing everything I did. Hermann did not say one unnecessary word to me all night. We worked hard, we communicated on every dish, and we got everything up onto the pass and out to the diners. It was probably the first evening he hadn't criticised me for something... anything. The stony silence made me nervous, like a storm was brewing underneath.

The final meal hit the pass, I wiped my brow and headed out the back for a few deep breaths of fresh air. I was sitting on a crate out the back of the restaurant when Hermann appeared. 'Luke,' he said.

I stood up. 'Yes, Mr Schneider.'

He put his arm around my shoulders and said, 'You didn't think you could do it, but you did. Good job chef.' Then he walked back inside.

It might not seem like much, but that was the best words of encouragement he ever gave me in four fucking years. Of course two weeks later I was on the same section and he ripped shreds off me for a string of cock-ups. But that didn't matter. That first night on the grill was a great test of my mettle as a chef. Hermann threw me in the deep end and I managed to come up for air unscathed by the end of the night.

Hermann doesn't remember that night, but he told me, 'I wouldn't have put you on the stove on a busy night if I didn't think you had the capability of doing it. If I did praise you on that night then you must have done a fantastic job. If it was your first night next to me and you did it successfully, then to me that was a very big step up for an apprentice.'

It was a defining moment. Sure, it seems like just a pat on the back, but Hermann never complimented the chefs. That evening it

CHECK CHEF

all became clear to me; I knew what I was going to do. It wasn't as if I was god's gift to cooking. Not at all. It simply meant I was a chef. I could handle it. I could actually do it. I wasn't a superstar in the kitchen, but I could cook. Check chef.

Incredibly, I ended up spending five years with Hermann.

I still had a lot to learn, and the reality was, to even get to that moment was a challenge in itself. It all started long before that evening, back in the Mangan family home in the Melbourne suburb of Forrest Hill.

2

FAMILY FEAST

I guess I grew up like many Aussie kids: middle class family in the 'burbs. Of course, with the Mangans being of Irish Catholic descent, there were quite a few of us. I'm the youngest of seven, all boys—my poor, poor mother.

Up until the autumn of 1970, my family lived in the regional Victorian town of Heathcote, known for its pink cliffs that were revealed during the gold rush mining period of the 1880s. Now, it's also one of my favourite regions in Australia for Shiraz. But the country life my family knew changed when my dad, William James Mangan, the bank manager at the Old Bank in Heathcote, took up an offer to be transferred to the big smoke of Melbourne. The role was to be bank manager of The Commercial Bank of Australia.

Mum, Marie Una Mangan, was a trained nurse, but Dad's big break allowed her to hang up the dress, apron and cap to take up a full time nursing gig—raising a house full of rowdy boys. Meanwhile Dad joined the throng of Melbourne's white collars and balanced the books.

Dad was as firm with his staff as he was with us kids. When I was about ten, Mum took me into Dad's work in Footscray. Mum wanted to do some shopping on her own and Dad and I were going to meet up with her somewhere for lunch. So I hung out in his office upstairs above the bank. I remember, when we both walked down the stairs to leave for lunch, seeing all these people queuing up to be served, but there were only two bank tellers on. Dad walked into the middle of the room and he did his 'nana. He was yelling 'where are the bloody bank tellers, get me three more bank tellers out here immediately, look at all the customers out here.' All the customers in the room cheered and applauded him.

It's funny, but I always remember that incident whenever I see the service side of things go wrong in a restaurant. It was the middle of the day and all the tellers had gone out for lunch, but all the customers were there, frustrated as hell with the lack of service. Even Dad knew back then that it doesn't matter what line of business you're in: if your service lets you down then your business will fail.

Within two weeks of the family leaving country Victoria's fresh air to set up a nest in Forrest Hill, I was born. On 6 May, to be precise. I'm the lucky number seven in a haggle of Mangan brothers: Shaun, Paul, Timothy, Michael, Matthew, David and finally yours truly—just sixteen years between us.

I asked Mum what sort of kid I was and she said, 'You were a good baby, a real happy kid, but you always had an answer for everything.' Some things never change.

Mum and Dad had a typical four-bedroom brick house built for them in the suburb of Forrest Hill, about 17 kilometres east of Melbourne's business district. Located in a dead-end street, our family home was the perfect setting for a pack of boys who loved the outdoors. Growing up in a house full of boys certainly plays a role in shaping what sort of person you become. For one, you soon develop an uncanny knack to talk back at people and give a bit of lip. You have to learn to hold your own and stand up for yourself; there's nowhere to hide in a pack that big. I'm not suggesting we were a pack of wild dogs; no doubt we were the same as any young lads finding their place on earth.

By the time I started to became a coherent kid running around and causing chaos there were only four of us at home: Michael, David, Matthew and me. Everyone says the youngest is a spoilt little brat. Well, I can tell you I certainly wasn't that. Except maybe for the brat part. I guess if being spoilt was getting all the hand-me-down used clothes, with a few holes in them that add 'character', then I'm guilty as charged. Clothes probably didn't hold up as well in those days, not because they were poorly made back then, but because in those days kids spent every waking minute outside in the sunshine, in the rain, in any conditions until Mum hollered for dinner. When I was a kid we were busy rolling around in the mud and if we managed a few scrapes and scratches on knees and elbows we wore them like badges of honour.

My brothers and I would practically hold the street to ransom. On hot summer days we'd pretty much close it down so we could play cricket on the road, kick to kick, chasing games or ride our bikes. There were even paddocks down the end with horses. If we saw a car, we'd grab the stumps from each end and move them out of the way until the car was gone, then we'd take over again.

Food was central in our household. We never dined in hatted restaurants or anything like that, but food brought all of us together. We'd sit around a large table with big bowls in the centre to share.

It was a communal environment with very simple, but well-cooked dishes. It undoubtedly sowed the seed of my philosophy of simple but flavoursome food. That warming, loving, hearty food shared at the table that takes you away from all of the troubles in the world and delivers a full belly and a happy heart.

Mum was the queen of stews, stocks and soups. Her trifle and custard weren't half-bad either. She was a genius at balancing cost, nutrition and flavour. She could teach a few chefs a thing or two about controlling your food costs and getting everything out of all your produce too.

There really wasn't money for luxuries. Dad ended up working four jobs at times; besides being a bank manager, he worked three other jobs at the weekend as well. So Mum always used to buy food in bulk. In those days there was this big warehouse, like a fruit barn, and Mum would go there with my nana and auntie and buy cases of oranges and apples.

We always had stewed fruit and custard for dessert. The main meals were mainly different mince dishes and, now and then if we were lucky, a nice roast. Whenever I go home to visit Mum these days, she asks me what would I like her to cook for dinner. I always say 'just one of your roast dinners and pudding thanks Mum.' They're hard to beat.

Mum was very loving. She always had breakfast on the table and lunch packed before school, and when we'd get home Mum was there in the kitchen with baked bread, some sort of soup, a hot cake… you name it. She really sparked my interest in food, and from a young age I was pulling at her apron wanting to get my hands dirty and cook something. Perhaps my favourite thing in the kitchen was making the Never Fail Cake... which oddly I managed to stuff up once, but I was only 13 so give me a fair go! The Never Fail Cake was one that mum and I would cook together. It was a basic sponge cake really: flour, milk, eggs, sugar and then flavourings like grated orange or lemon rind. You can't go wrong... apparently.

According to Mum I'd hover around her prodding at things in the kitchen and asking questions like 'What's this Mum? How did you make that? Can I do that?'

I asked her what she remembers and she told me, 'You were so bloody messy in the kitchen and you didn't like cleaning up your own mess either, so guess who had to clean it up?'

Mum and I used to bake a lot of bread too. We had a pre-mix bread product, where basically all you do is add the yeast and water and you're away. But for me the best part was proving it above the gas heater in the lounge room. I used to sit on the lounge and watch it eagerly, waiting to get the bloody thing in the oven. That was a lot of fun.

Mum taught me that food isn't about showing off and being tricky, it's about simplicity, putting love into it and making it flavoursome.

She wasn't really the tough one; that was Dad. He was firm, but very fair. He worked bloody hard, and he expected his sons to follow suit. Every night he'd say 'why isn't he doing his homework?' If there was ever a breadwinner setting an example to us boys it was my Dad. He did whatever it took to put enough food on the table. He was a machine.

And although Mum was very tolerant, she was no shirker. She certainly kept us boys in line. She worked tirelessly in the engine room of our house to ensure we were well fed and well groomed. Can you imagine looking after eight males? Not only that, it was eight Mangans! She's an impressive and resilient woman. I remember one night where the exhaustion from manning the Mangan household spilled over... quite literally.

FAMILY FEAST

The whole family sat down at the table for another typical hearty feast. Mum had slaved away all day doing our washing, ironing and preparing a dinner for all the hungry grumbling Mangan tummies. She'd dished up one of her classic versions of sausage casserole with mash, carrots and brussels sprouts. As a kid, brussels sprouts were kind of an unnecessary evil on the plate, and it's no surprise because in those days you never did anything else with brussels sprouts except boil them.

My oldest brother Timmy was perhaps the biggest shit stirrer in the family, he loved it. So here we were about to dive headfirst into another Marie Mangan feast and Timmy looked at the sausages, carrot and brussels sprouts and said 'brussels sprouts? Not again, I'm not eating these.'

Mum must have been very tired that night and a bit fed up. She calmly got up, walked over to Timmy, picked up his plate and emptied it on his head.

There was stunned silence… then we all broke out into raucous laughter.

In one way or another Mum's food was really the thing that brought us all together. Every night we'd rush home from school in anticipation of something tasty on the kitchen bench awaiting our arrival. We'd wander through the front door sniffing the air to try and work out what Mum had cooked.

3

MINGY AND THE MISFITS

My problem was that I hated school. I was useless at it and had no interest in improving my grades either. I went to a very conservative Christian Brothers school in Box Hill, Victoria, called St Leo's College. It's a school that all my brothers attended, which made moving there in grade four my worst nightmare. In grade four, you're about nine or ten years old, and six of my brothers had already tainted the views of the school's administration. For better or worse the Mangans had a bit of a name in the school.

I was an awkward little kid; I was short, skinny, I was bloody cross-eyed and I had these thick Coke-bottle glasses. As a result I was picked on a bit. In grade four I met a guy named Chris 'Lynchy' Lynch, who's been my best mate ever since—some 30-odd years now. Compared to me Chris was a pretty big kid; he was always pretty good at sport and he certainly didn't mind the odd scrap either. We both came from fairly similar backgrounds of big Catholic families with similar parenting. His father was a magistrate and a fairly disciplined man, not unlike my dad. Both of us were expected to do well at school and work hard, but we were both dreamers and neither of us had any interest in being there.

I can't recall when we first actually met but Chris has a better memory than me. He told me 'We used to play Aussie rules at lunchtime and I always noticed that you rarely got the ball. So every second ball I got, I'd chuck it to you to give you a bit of a kick. I guess the friendship stemmed from that.'

We were only young kids then, but it wasn't long before we realised we had similar views about school. We just clicked.

By the time we were in our early teens, our lack of interest in school had become so dire that we were wagging on a regular basis. For the most part it was Chris and I, but for a period there were four of us who constantly cut class: Chris 'Lynchy' Lynch, John 'Dalts' Dalton, 'Boofer' Merritt and me—who was given the nickname 'Mingy'. We were basically a bunch of misfits. We just didn't fit into the regular mould of what a student should be at St Leo's College. We ran our own race and bucked the system a fair bit.

Often Chris and I would wag school and go and sit down by the creek in an area Chris called 'The Mingy Spot'. We used to go down there for lunch with no intention of going back to school. We were pretty happy enjoying the sunshine, sitting under the trees and daydreaming. It was really just an escape from reality. It wasn't long before the teachers caught on and found out where we'd go to skip class. In an effort to change our errant ways they banned us from certain parts of the oval. We were also warned that if we tried it again we would face severe punishment. From that day on, being at school was like being in a correctional facility and it marked the beginning of our contempt for authority.

One day Chris and I managed to get 'past the guards' and went across the road to get fish and chips and head down to The Mingy Spot for lunch. The teachers knew exactly what we were up to and eagerly awaited our return. As we came back over the river our number was up. We were accused of leaving the school grounds and smoking cigarettes—something we never, ever did. We both ended up getting the cane and detention. We were filthy about it because we never, ever smoked. As for wagging? Well, guilty as charged Your Honour.

Sadly though, we never learned our lesson. We were on a wild ride to oblivion and no amount of common sense or discipline was going to stop us. At the age of 13 we went on a school camp to Point Leo down in the Mornington Peninsula. The teachers had organised some sort of orientation course where we broke off into small groups with a map and a series of clues in order to find our way to the campsite. The four of us misfits started the course with all the intentions in the world to go and do it correctly. Typically though, not one of us knew how to read the clues or the map and we had no idea what we were doing. We decided to try and wing it by taking a short cut from point A to point B, but of course we got lost. So, as usual, we did our own thing and decided to sit by the riverbed. We just hung out, laughed, swore, planned practical jokes and mucked around like a pack of idiots while all the other kids went on this huge expedition. After a few hours the school van drove past us and went around the corner. I remember Chris saying 'Holy shit, there's the school bus, we should follow it back to camp.'

Little did we know we were only 300 metres from the campgrounds the whole time. More importantly, the teachers had seen us by the river and knew what we were up to. They left us to our devices but were listening to us the whole time. We certainly weren't the sharpest tools in the shed. For our troubles we were banned from a lot of the activities during the camp. But we didn't care; we wore that sort of punishment like a badge of honour.

We just wanted to do things our way, but often our way caused a bit of trouble. On one occasion Chris and I found a key lying outside in the playground, which we tried on practically every door in the school. Soon enough we found out it was the key to the school canteen. We thought we'd hit the jackpot. We broke in and helped ourselves. We ate like kings for a day, but yet again detention loomed around the corner for our actions. We were hopeless, and as a result my grades were nothing short of appalling.

My Physical Education grades were good, up around 76 out of 100 at their best, but as soon as you stuck me behind a desk I fell to pieces. Mathematics was my most hated subject. I never understood what was going on and I'm surprised I managed to get the grades that appear on my records. For the majority of my schooling I was averaging between 22–30 out of 100 for Mathematics. To be honest I think the Brothers were being way too generous.

Chris Lynch seems to remember those days much better than me and told me, 'As far as academia goes you were horrible Luke. Remember when a Brother felt sorry for you and tried to help you? The tough old bugger, Brother Hewitt, but I think he had a bit of time for you. On one occasion he actually gave you all the answers for a Maths exam prior to the test to try and help you out. But you still failed the test!'

I never managed a pass mark for general Science during my entire schooling life, but I got bloody close with a 45 out of 100 once.

English wasn't much better but at least I managed the occasional pass mark. I generally hovered between 40–50 out of 100 with an all-time high of 55 out of 100 in year eight. A rare highlight was a massive 65 out of 100 for Geography in my final year. Sadly though, it was a one-off and I pretty much averaged around the 30s for that too.

Mum and Dad decided enough was enough and they got me a tutor to combat my errant ways. A classmate of my brother Matt at St Leo's, Dennis Carney, got the gig. Dennis is now a very well respected doctor at Melbourne's St Vincent's Hospital, but sadly tutoring was just a waste of time and money. Not through any fault of Dennis; I was just never going to give it the attention it required. Even with my tutoring I'd rock up for a test, answer a few questions and then pretty much sit there daydreaming until the test was over.

As a result of my lack of discipline I spent 95 per cent of the time outside the classroom in the corridor for disrupting the class. There were things I'd do, like screw up pieces of paper and throw them at the teacher and pretend it wasn't me. I'd make up stupid jokes, dish up smartarse comments or draw stupid pictures and pass them around the class. I guess my all-time favourite was throwing around paper planes, which drove some of the kids mad.

I never, ever did my homework. I remember in form one the teacher asked us to read a few chapters of a book overnight. The following day the teacher asked me to explain what happened in chapter ten. I replied 'I don't think my copy has a chapter ten, Sir!'

Chris and I sat next to each other in Maths. The classroom had a window that tilted and looked out onto the corridor. We'd always make sure we got the seats under that window because more often than not one of us would get chucked out of class for some silly reason and we'd be made to sit outside that window. One time Chris got kicked out for throwing a paper plane that hit the teacher on the back of the head. It was a great shot, but he got sent out to sit in the corridor. I started throwing screwed up bits of paper, with stupid messages on them, out of the window at Chris. One of them hit him in the eye and the two of us burst out laughing. So I got kicked out too. The teacher was getting pretty tired of our routine and it had obviously all bottled up inside him. He was screaming at us and in venting his frustration he lashed out and whacked Chris in the head. Chris and I looked at each other and burst out laughing again. It was all just a big joke to us.

There was one saving grace in my school years. I started doing a subject called Woodwork. We had to build pencil boxes, wooden ornaments and things like that. I've actually still got the pencil box I built all those years ago. Woodwork was a great escape because it meant I wasn't sitting behind a fucking desk and while I didn't excel at it, I enjoyed the challenge of using my hands and creating something. I think that sparked a bit of a creative element in me.

My Woodwork teacher, Mr Neal, was great. He was probably the first teacher who saw something in me. What exactly that was I'm not entirely sure, but he realised that it was probably first time I was actually enjoying something at school rather than making a nuisance of myself.

One day, during class, he pulled me aside and asked, 'Now Luke, what do you want to do when you leave school?'

'Well, I don't know, Sir,' I replied.

He said, 'What do you do at home, or what do you enjoy doing?'

'Mum's a really good cook and I actually cook with her a lot.'

'What sort of things do you cook?' he asked.

'Bread, cakes, cookies… all sorts of things.'

'Why don't you bring in a cake you made with your mum, and instead of doing Woodwork you can ice the cake here at school and feed all the kids in the class?'

So I thought *okay, I will*. I went off home, and I was pretty excited. It may well be the only school project that I've ever been enthused about doing… and I was eager to impress.

So Mum and I got up early before school the next day and made my favourite: the Mangan family orange cake. I took the cake in with all the ingredients to make the icing, and when it came to woodwork class I basically put on a show for everyone. Sure, all I did was make the icing and ice the cake, but the excitement and anticipation from everyone in the room was a bit intoxicating. They loved it and all anyone would talk about was what I would bring in next time.

For the first time I had a taste of what it was like to achieve a goal. It gave me a bit of confidence and I realised I could create something that people enjoyed. Even more importantly, I realised it was the first thing I ever enjoyed doing at school.

Mr Neal noticed too. 'Luke, I think should look into becoming a chef, it's obviously something you enjoy, and you can cook.'

By this time I was almost 15 and nearly old enough to leave school legally.

Like most school kids at that age it was a requirement to do a fortnight's work experience to help guide us into a career. I still really didn't know what I wanted to do but had an opportunity to go and do some work experience at the restaurant my older brother Michael was working at in South Yarra. It was called Two Faces.

MINGY AND THE MISFITS

At the time I had no idea that the owner, Hermann Schneider, was one of the best chefs in the country and his restaurant, Two Faces, was arguably one of Australia's finest.

It was a bit of a rude awakening for me. For the entire two weeks all I did was peel onions and wash potatoes. I hated it. But compared to school I saw it as a bit of an escape. Nothing was more painful than maths, absolutely nothing. After two weeks of peeling fucking vegetables I went back to school and, to be honest, things weren't any better. I hated turning up and my bad attitude was taking a toll on my teachers. No doubt my antics were also pissing off the other students who actually *were* interested in a formal education. The school basically came to the conclusion that the best thing really was for me to move on.

Chris was no longer at school either. He'd been asked to leave about six months earlier and his departure had a major impact on me. He was my ally, he was my best mate and without him around I probably started to fuck up even more, if that was possible.

Mum and Dad talked about getting me into another school for a fresh start, but Dad really wanted me to stay there. He believed St Leo's was the one place you could get a strong education. All my other brothers had received their education there. But the reality was, I was 15 and it was time to get out of school. They weren't going to put up with my shit any longer.

Wanting to leave school was one thing, getting the all-clear from my parents was another thing altogether. I knew Dad would be totally against it. Although two of my other brothers had left school at 15, my dad believed success rode on the back of a full formal education. I knew he'd be a hard sell. My only chance of swaying them was by going to Mum first. She was often pretty sympathetic to my hatred of school, but I knew I'd have to do some heavy groundwork to get her across the line.

One afternoon I joined her in the kitchen and simply said, 'Mum, I want to leave school.'

She put the knife down and looked at me. 'No, Luke, you're too young.'

'But Mum, I suck at a school,' I replied.

She wasn't convinced, so over the next week I basically nagged her until she couldn't take any more. She realised that if I wasn't happy at school and I was causing so much trouble and wagging then perhaps I was better off not being there. When my report card came back Mum and Dad had a couple of talks with the master of the school and they both knew it just wasn't going to work.

Mum and Dad sat me down. Mum said, 'If you leave school you must have a job to go to first, you're not sitting around on your backside doing nothing.'

With two weeks of work experience under my belt, it seemed natural that getting a job as an apprentice chef would solve all of my problems. What else was I going to do? Cheffing seemed the only thing that could save me from going back to school. So I rang Hermann and asked if I could start an apprenticeship.

'No,' he said bluntly.

Well, that wasn't the response I was hoping for.

'What the bloody hell do you want to do this for? You have no idea what you'd be getting yourself into,' he said.

Hermann had seen his fair share of chefs who started with a lot of enthusiasm, but when they had to knuckle down and do the hard yards, they became disinterested and left the industry. Some things never change.

'People don't realise how hard it is to be a chef, Luke,' he continued. 'You are signing up for four years of very hard work, do you really want this?'

'Yes, Mr Schneider, I'm a very hard worker,' I replied.

That's it. That's all I had. I'm a very hard worker? That was my big pitch to one of Australia's best chefs?

He said he'd think about it.

According to John Lepp he and Hermann had a bit of a debate as to whether I could cut the mustard in the kitchen. He told me, 'We weren't sure you had the mettle for it.'

Hermann asked John what he thought, and he said 'Well, Luke's brother Michael was good, so he comes from good stock. Why not give him a whirl and see how tough he is?'

A few days later Hermann rang me with the news I was hoping for. He said, 'I'll give you an apprenticeship, but don't you let me down.'

It was the best news I'd ever heard.

That night during dinner I raised it with my parents. 'I've landed this great apprenticeship at Two Faces, so I can leave school now.'

Dad's immediate response was, 'Luke, what about school? I really want you to finish school.'

I said, 'This is the best restaurant in Australia. Come on, Dad, I'm going to be a chef!'

Dad looked at Mum. Mum looked at Dad. I think they both realised then that this was a real opportunity for me. So he basically gave me an ultimatum.

'You start your apprenticeship at Two Faces and you finish your apprenticeship there. The minute you leave that apprenticeship you're back at school, no arguments.'

Dad was always very firm like that.

'Is it a deal, do you promise?' he asked.

'Yep, okay, it's a deal,' I replied.

Truth be told, the apprenticeship didn't mean a whole lot to me. I had no idea what I was getting myself into. I certainly didn't think I was going to be a great chef. I still didn't even know what I wanted to be, I was just glad I wasn't in school any more.

4

DONE DEAL, BUT THE DEVIL'S IN THE DETAIL

I woke up at 6am. It was cold and I was tired. In my snoozy state I could hear Mum calling out to me: 'Luke, time to get up, you've got a big day today.' She must have said it about ten times.

After two weeks of work experience at Two Faces I had a fair idea of how my day was going to unfold. Going back to sleep seemed like a better option.

I finally got up and walked bleary-eyed into the kitchen. Mum had my breakfast on the table and Dad was already dressed for work and halfway through his breakfast. This was the first day of my chef apprenticeship and I had to be up even earlier than I needed to be for school.

At that stage in my life I didn't really know what hard work was. I was a typical teen: bored, disinterested, lazy. Apart from the work experience, the only job I'd had was pumping petrol at my Uncle Geoff's petrol station. I guess I was about 13 at the time. On Saturdays Dad would take me there and then pick me up after six full hours of work. I was paid $25 a day to pump the fuel and mow the lawns. That was it. Of course one time during the school holidays I went and stayed with my brother Tim in Sydney. He was a bricklayer, so I went to work with him and spent a whole week picking bricks up, wheeling them somewhere else and then lifting them out of the wheelbarrow again. I wouldn't call it a job I wanted to do, and it certainly didn't feel like a holiday. So really, I had no idea what working full time was like.

I got ready, and soon enough Dad and I were in the car and on the way to Two Faces for my 7am start. We pulled up at the restaurant and it was still pitch black outside. 'Good luck,' he said. 'You'll be fine, just do a good job at whatever you do, okay?' I shut the car door and made my way in.

I was bloody nervous. Thankfully I had done the work experience already so I felt like at the very least I knew the chefs and my way around the kitchen. But by the time I started at Two Faces my brother Michael had moved on, so I was going into the war zone as a lone soldier.

When I walked in no one said a word to me. They were all busy working and I felt like I was invisible. I'd soon learn that no one was invisible in that kitchen and there would be nowhere to hide. Nowhere. I made my way to the staff room, put on my brand new chef whites and awkwardly ventured into the kitchen.

Hermann Schneider and head chef John Lepp welcomed me to the team, and before I knew it, I was shoved out the back into the prep kitchen to peel prawns, peel potatoes and wash dishes.

DONE DEAL, BUT THE DEVIL'S IN THE DETAIL

Welcome back to hell.

My apprenticeship started at Two Faces in South Yarra, but soon enough my time was shared between there and Roesti Bistro, Hermann's other restaurant in the city. Two Faces was fine dining in every sense, but Roesti Bistro fed the city's white collars with good honest bistro fare.

The kitchen at Two Faces was tiny. About six or seven chefs squeezed into a space not much bigger than a domestic kitchen to try and dish up arguably the best food in the country. Looking back now, I can't believe we did it. There were two parts to the tiny kitchen: a prep and wash area out the back and the service kitchen, where all the magic happened before everything was whisked away to feed Melbourne's foodie elite.

Being the new kid on the block with no skills whatsoever, I spent most of my days in the prep and wash area with Bobby the butcher. Sounds like a nickname for a serial killer, and on first impressions he filled the brief, but Bobby the butcher was a real nice bloke. He'd looked after the meat and fish butchery section at Two Faces for 20 years by the time I arrived, and I was only 15. He'd been there for my entire life, and then some.

During the early days they'd send me home at about 8pm because I was physically exhausted, and the kitchen was so tiny I'd simply be in the way. Of course, it wasn't long before they had me on the 7am until midnight doubles that the industry is renowned for.

If it weren't for both my parents there is no way in living hell I would have finished my apprenticeship. Dad was pretty committed to making it work. He never said much, he just did things. He'd always take me to the train station at 7am to get me on the train to work. He'd then go to work all day and end up picking me up at 11pm as well.

Whenever I was struggling with it all, Mum was there to listen and talk about it. I can't tell you the amount of times I came home completely destroyed. I'd be in tears, I'd want to throw it all in, but Mum would always be there to talk me out of it.

I'd come home saying 'I'm not going back there, I hate it, it's too hard, the hours are too long.'

Mum would sit me down and say 'Well don't think of now, think of what could happen, and what advantages you could get when you are older. One day all this hard work will be worth it.'

My problem was that I just wasn't a quick learner, plus I didn't listen. If someone showed me the correct way to dice an onion, for instance, I couldn't do it right until I'd prepped it a dozen times. I was hopeless.

The apprenticeship was almost worse than school. Almost. I certainly hated every day of it. It was long hours, physical hours on your feet in hot conditions with flames, ovens, steamers and fryers. It didn't take long for me to find out about foot rot and chef chafe, two hazards of the trade.

Like many chefs in Melbourne, I completed the theory part of my apprenticeship at William Angliss College, a TAFE institute. I was just as useless at cooking school as I was at school. I couldn't concentrate and wasn't interested in the theory side of things. I was mucking up again, being the class clown by throwing pieces of screwed up paper and basically being an idiot.

The only thing that got me through cooking school was that I was top of the class in practical: I'd make all the sauces and stocks really well.

I guess I was this young, cocky and confident kid because I was working in one of the best restaurants in the country. Because of that, everyone would come up to me and ask 'how do you do this' and

DONE DEAL, BUT THE DEVIL'S IN THE DETAIL

'is this right' during the practical part of the class. It bolstered my confidence, perhaps a little too much. No one came to me for help during normal school, that's for sure, so this was a kind of revelation.

There's no doubt Two Faces' head chef John Lepp was the driving force behind that. He took me under his wing a bit and stuck up for me a lot too. He was always very good to me, and a great motivator. He would teach me how to make everything, like all the mother sauces, before we'd do them in practical in TAFE.

If it weren't for John Lepp I probably wouldn't have finished TAFE, or my apprenticeship. The same goes for Mick Kelly, the head chef at Roesti Bistro, who was one of only a few who finished his entire apprenticeship under Hermann. Little did I know at the time I would be the other chosen one! Because of John I was getting a 90 per cent mark in my practical, and somehow I scratched together a 50 per cent mark in my theory too. John, one of the best chefs I have ever worked under, had extraordinary patience with me and was a fantastic teacher.

Nowadays, the TAFE system just confuses me. I wonder why we are teaching our kids the béchamel, the waldorf salad, the caesar salad and those sorts of things. It's good for them to know these classics but Australia's cuisine has changed so much in the last 20 years. I'd like to see more of an Asian influence on the courses taught to apprentices. When I was going to TAFE, I'd never even heard of a masterstock, let alone what it was used for.

Back at Two Faces, I was still uncomfortable, and I was still fucking things up. No one really spoke to me, apart from yelling at me if I wasn't doing things right. I was certainly never commended if I did do things well. It would take me a whole day to pick a box of beans, and it just wasn't sinking in how hard I actually needed to work.

LUKE MANGAN

Hermann preferred virtual silence in the kitchen. He believed if you knew your job, and the chef working next to you knew their job, it should work seamlessly without any verbal communication. He once said that a service in a kitchen is a little bit like the intensity of an operating theatre. He always admired how surgeons and the operating nurse worked together.

'The surgeon hardly has to say anything, because the nurse knows exactly what the surgeon requires to get the job done. That's very much like cooking,' he told me.

His point was that when you have three or four dishes to plate up at the same time and you have to tell someone every one or two minutes what they should be doing, it's exhausting and the evening won't be as productive as it can be. On top of that you have waiters talking to you, asking for dishes, and it's chaos. It makes sense to shut up, focus and communicate when it's necessary.

Of course that didn't stop him from shouting the house down if you fucked up. I was always running behind and as a result I used to cop it pretty hard. Hermann might have seemed like a tough bastard at that time, and he was, but he certainly turned boys into men pretty quickly. You soon learned that whatever your role was, you had to focus and get it done properly.

There was obviously a method to Hermann's madness, as he's had a number of proteges who have gone onto greater things. In my time alone at Two Faces, Teage Ezard and Guy Grossi were a part of the kitchen crew. Being flogged every shift by Hermann in those early days became the foundation of my great friendship with Guy Grossi that has spanned some 20-odd years now.

It was certainly a tough environment and, although I hated it, I was starting to get in a rhythm. It dawned on me that if I just put my

DONE DEAL, BUT THE DEVIL'S IN THE DETAIL

head down and worked hard, I didn't get yelled at and all was good. If you weren't pulling your weight then you were in a lot of trouble and you wouldn't hold your job for long. It was that simple. When you do an apprenticeship with someone like Hermann you have to work damn hard. If you didn't, well, you knew where the door was.

5

FINDING MY FEET, BUT LANDING ON MY HEAD

Hermann never wore a chef's jacket in the kitchen. He had this long white doctor's coat that he wore and these big old black-rimmed doctor's glasses too.

Every day as midday approached, we all feared that moment when the gold Volvo rolled up and a tornado blew through the door to dissect all the work we'd already done. It would be right near service and he'd come in and spend 15 minutes going through my mise en place, and say 'get rid of that, what's this doing here, that's no good, change that—*boom, boom, boom!*' I would have to do it all again, because I just never got anything right to the standard required.

One morning we were all busily preparing for the lunch trade. Hermann was still at the markets and all the staff were talking and laughing.

FINDING MY FEET, BUT LANDING ON MY HEAD

All of a sudden the familiar white doctor's coat and black-rimmed glasses came flying through the door, with arms waving everywhere. Suddenly there were kitchen staff running in all directions.

And then we realised it was actually the sommelier Curtis Marsh, who had snuck out the back, slipped into Hermann's spare jacket and donned a pair of his black-rimmed glasses. He had everyone fooled! It was brilliant. Order was soon restored—but of course we had to knuckle down quick smart, Hermann was still to come in.

After about a year my working week was usually split between the two venues. A few nights a week I'd be in the galley of Two Faces doing menial tasks and a hell of a lot of prep, but during the lunch trade I was given greater responsibility to bash out the bistro food in the hard-and-fast rush hour at Roesti Bistro.

That place allowed me to understand the meaning of a deadline. The lunch trade was fast and furious, but Hermann's high standards still had to be met. So it certainly sharpened up my skills pretty quick.

Hermann was born in Switzerland and trained in the old-school formal European chef training. He came to Australia, with a number of top European chefs, to be part of the team that catered for the 1956 Melbourne Olympics. Australia became his home from that moment.

He was tough, and he believed the only way to get the best out of a chef was to make him tough too. That's how I really cut my teeth and experienced the pressures of a commercial kitchen: during the throes of a busy service at Roesti Bistro. Hermann threw me in the deep end.

The average lunch service meant you were cooking for roughly 90 people within a two-hour period. I was only in my second year, but all of a sudden I was literally running the downstairs grill during lunch service.

The menu was deliberately concise but packed a punch on flavour. Essentially there were a few main dishes: the bratwurst sausage, the deep-fried whiting in beer batter, the beef paillard and the grilled chicken. All were served with roesti potatoes, which are basically Swiss fried spuds.

I know that might sound simple but when you do 90 a day you have to have your shit together—especially when you are only 16 or 17 years of age and you have the great Swiss shark circling. He had a pretty sharp eye and he knew what he wanted, and what he expected of you.

The hotbox at Roesti Bistro housed the bread or Swiss cheese tarts from the day's trade, and the waiters used to raid it after service. Typical waiters, always hungry and looking for scraps! Of course, when you are in the kitchen cooking, it's pretty hard to go hungry: you're always trying, tasting and testing your food. A chef who sends food out without checking the seasoning and the balance of flavours and ensures everything is perfect is a chef who's heading in only one direction: down.

Hermann and his late wife Faye would often have lunch after service at Roesti Bistro, and Hermann was very good at counting how many Swiss cheese tarts were left. One day, one of the waiters stole the last tart. Hermann had just sat down and said 'I'll have the cheese tart.' Someone had to go out and tell him there were none left.

Hermann knew there was one left over from lunch and so he went into a rage. 'Who stole the bloody cheese tart?'

'I don't know, Mr Schneider,' I replied. Of course I knew who it was: those damn waiters!

FINDING MY FEET, BUT LANDING ON MY HEAD

'You better tell me who it is, Luke!'

'But I don't know who took it, Mr Schneider,' I said.

It went on for days, and the waiters owed me big time!

Life was changing. I still hated my job, but I was getting more confident and I was starting to grow up too. Chris Lynch and I got our hands on some fake IDs, and it changed our lives in an instant. The first nightclub I ever went to was a place called Barbarella's, in Fitzroy. Lynchy used to come and pick me up at Two Faces at about 11pm when I knocked off. We must have been about 16 or 17 at the time, but armed with our fake IDs we'd roll our way in and then paint the town red.

One time I met Lynchy at a nightclub after I'd finished work. I turned up with all my chef knives. Lynchy said to me, 'What the hell are you doing with them? You can't carry knives around in public.'

'I had to bring them home. I can't leave them at work,' I replied.

I was underage but they let me put my knives into the cloakroom. Can't imagine a nightclub letting you check your knives in at the door these days!

Just as I was getting into a routine, life was about to change again. Hermann sold Two Faces to a consortium, and not long after he offloaded Roesti Bistro to Geoff Strang, who was the proprietor of a French bistro in Richmond called Les Halles at the time.

Hermann had his sights set on opening Two Faces at Delgany Country House Hotel in the southern seaside town of Portsea. It meant that eventually the majority of the kitchen crew, including me, would be moving south for work.

In the couple of months between the closure of Two Faces and the opening of Delgany, I did a small stint at my brother Michael's place,

Flinder's Bakery. I may never have ended up at Portsea at all, because one night after work at Flinder's Bakery I nearly killed myself in a car accident.

I'd finished my shift and jumped in the car to collect a load of pizzas for all of the chefs. It'd been a long night and I was pretty tired, and for one reason or another I got lost on the way. I ended up driving down a dirt road in god-knows-where, and being a typical 18-year-old with a license to thrill behind the wheel of a tinny little Toyota station wagon, I put the pedal to the metal and was flying along. I was way over the speed limit when I suddenly hit a ditch and lost control of the vehicle. I swerved from one side of the road to the other and hit the gutter. The car flipped and I rammed into a tree. The car had landed on its roof and here I was semi-conscious, upside down and in the middle of nowhere.

Thank God the car flipped, because the passenger side took the full impact of the tree. A nanosecond either way might have spelled the end of me.

Somehow I came to my senses, undid my seat belt, fell to the ground and eventually crawled out of the smoking wreck. I checked myself all over and, unbelievably, didn't have any cuts or bruises on me. God I was lucky. Adrenaline was pumping through my veins and I could feel my heart hammering against my chest. I really didn't know what to do and I started to panic. I didn't have a mobile phone in those days and it was just starting to dawn on me what had actually happened.

Sure the accident didn't kill me, but I thought Dad might once he saw the car: it was a write-off. I was shitting myself and decided to sit on the side of the road. I took a few deep breaths, then got up and had a look around. In the distance I could see a small light. I made my way towards this weird two-storey house. I banged on the door, but there was no response. Maybe I was delirious at the time, but I climbed up a fucking tree to the level where the light was on, to get the owner's attention.

Inside there was this really old couple. I think I scared the hell out of them. Can you imagine? It's 1am, in the middle of nowhere and here's some 18-year-old idiot in their tree screaming out nonsense to them.

After explaining what had happened, the old lady let me in the house. Her husband was sitting on a big chair in the lounge room with some sort of respiratory mask on that was wired up to an oxygen tank. It was like I was in some sort of twisted horror film. That poor old couple. Thankfully they were lovely and let me use the phone to call my brother Michael, who I was living with at the time.

Michael got in his car immediately and picked me up. I was freaking out because I realised that the hardest part now was how to explain it all to Dad. He was not going to be happy about it. Michael kept telling me not to worry about it, and that he'd talk to Dad. 'It'll be alright, Luke,' he kept saying.

I don't remember much of what happened when we got home, but I know that Mick stuck up for me that night and he explained to Dad that it was all just an accident. I think he prevented Dad from giving me a right bollocking.

The next day, once we all settled down we realised that I'd nearly killed myself. I could quite easily have been another statistic on Victorian roads. What an idiot. I was young, speeding on a dirt road and stupid. I was very, very lucky to survive it.

6

SANCTITY OF THE SEASIDE

It was the summer of 1988 when I moved down to the seaside town of Portsea for the opening of Two Faces at Delgany Country House Hotel. The restaurant, which was named after a village in County Wicklow, Ireland, by a previous owner, was set on the coast and soon became the heartbeat of the food scene. It was a pretty exciting time in my life. I was 18, starting to gain a bit of confidence and Portsea was a real hotspot for young party-goers during summer. Although it was busy every day, the weekends saw a procession of university students eager to let their hair down: not unlike America's spring break in Florida, but with a bit more class perhaps!

Portsea was like paradise. There was sun, surf and plenty of gorgeous women too. Problem was, I spent most of my time in the kitchen.

SANCTITY OF THE SEASIDE

The lifestyle consisted of working all day until midnight then hitting the pub for drinks, getting a few hours' sleep then doing it all again. If you got a day off you felt like you'd hit the jackpot.

It was like a rite of passage. When you work in a hard environment like that, if you don't go and blow off some steam after work then you start to build anxiety amongst the team. It's important to relax and unwind, and when you finish work at midnight, the 'unwinding' is usually living it large in a bar.

Unfortunately I drew the shortest straw quite often and had the unenviable job of doing the breakfast shift. You'd be getting up at 5:30am for a 6am start and often working through to midnight. The person who did the breakfast shift was given a two-hour break in the middle of the day to duck home and have a nap before joining everyone in the kitchen for the night service.

Once on the dreaded breakfast shift, I was slicing ham on the big meat slicer in preparation for the morning's service. I must have lost concentration: maybe I'd had a big night or maybe I was just unlucky, but I ended up putting the top of my fingers through the slicer. It was pretty nasty. There was blood everywhere, and at first I didn't really know the damage I'd done. I looked at my hand and you could see my finger bones. What a dreamer. I still have the scars.

The amount of chefs going through Delgany was amazing. It was like a merry-go-round as a procession of chefs gave it a shot, but the long hours saw them head back to Melbourne in no time.

Hermann's approach to cheffing had conditioned us to deal with anything, and the real bonus was having John Lepp as head chef down at Delgany as well. John didn't quite stay the distance at Delgany either, but he was the master of holding a team together when the shit hit the fan, while also getting the best out of each individual in the kitchen. And just as we'd experienced in South Yarra, there was really no measure given for not pulling your weight or sloppy workmanship either. It was serious business.

The kitchen at Delgany was as good as you could get. After dealing with the tiny kitchen at Two Faces in South Yarra, Delgany was a godsend. We had this big lovely space with all brand new stoves, new pots and pans and the best of everything: crockery, cutlery, silverware. It was incredible.

It was arguably one of the finest venues in Australia at the time, and was rewarded as such in 1990 with three chef's hats in *The Age Good Food Guide*—the highest accolade a restaurant can achieve in Australia.

I shared an apartment with a guy named Darren Barnett. I first met Darren back in the days when I was cleaning out the grease traps at Roesti Bistro. We became good mates. It was my first job, and for Darren, who was a country boy from Bendigo, it was his first job working in the big smoke. He's still one of my best mates and plies his trade at Sydney's much-adored Bistro Moncur. In fact, he worked a good few years for us at Salt.

We lived on the main street of Sorrento above a menswear store, which was next door to a butcher's shop. It was unreal. It was simply a matter of walking down the back stairs, into the butcher's and then back upstairs to cook a feast. When you're a young adult chef possibly the only thing better than living above a butcher's would be living above a bottle shop!

We ended up befriending the butcher. On the odd occasion we'd go drinking with him, then late at night we'd come home, he'd grab his keys and we'd get some meat and do a massive cook up.

We certainly had a lot of fun. The usual suspects were myself, Darren, John Lepp, a crazy Queenslander named Carl and, on the weekends, Curtis Marsh, who'd become a great mate while at we were at Two Faces and Roesti Bistro.

One night a whole group of us got so drunk, we decided to lay some mattresses on the stairs and do something we called 'dwarf throwing'. Darren is such a small thin guy, we'd grab him and throw him down the stairs. It was pretty harmless fun really and Darren didn't seem to mind. In fact I think he thoroughly enjoyed it.

Carl was mad, and a hell of a lot of fun too. Curtis used to tell us that Hermann was constantly furious with Carl because he was a big bumbling uncoordinated madman of a waiter. Carl was so large that he used to pivot from his hip as he put food down on the table. He was almost like a giant lever. I remember Curtis coming into the kitchen to tell me we had a big group of Japanese tourists in for dinner, and when Carl dropped off a plate at the table he'd pivot, then they would all respond and bow back at him.

Curtis was making a transition from being a sommelier to the wine wholesale-distribution industry at the time. He created a company called Select Vineyards, which saw him do a combination of consulting to restaurants doing wine lists, then selling wine day and night.

On weekends he'd head down to Sorrento to work at Delgany. He would bring down mixed dozens of wine for Darren and I from his clients. It was a real education. That was our 'Sorrento winter survival pack', which came in handy I can assure you. Of course we could clean up two dozen easily in a few days when we all got together. Those were the days.

Curtis gave me my first ever drink of wine, which fuelled my fascination for the stuff from that moment. When I was about 13 Mum and Dad had a house down at Flinders, and we'd go and stay there and have counter meals at the local pub. My Uncle Peter would come along and give me a Jelly Bean to drink. It's essentially ouzo, lemonade and grenadine. I must have been about 13 at the time, and he'd tell my parents it was just a red lemonade. Sure, it was only one or two, but I felt pretty special.

A few years later I had my 15th birthday at Two Faces with my entire family. Curtis Marsh served our table and asked if we'd like a pre-dinner drink, so I ordered a Jelly Bean. Curtis replied, 'Okay Luke, this is the last Jelly Bean you will drink in your life. From now on you are going to drink wine.'

We had so much fun that Delgany is almost a blur. We worked extremely hard and when given time off we played even harder.

My fondest memories of that time were the progressive dinners we'd put on. Everyone was passionate about food and wine, so the idea was to go to each person's house where they would put on a course for everyone. Then you'd move onto the next house, and so on. More often than not we'd start off at our place for canapés, and then we'd move over to John Lepp's for entrées, and then across to Carl's for mains.

Although I loved it, I was hopeless. John Lepp loves to tell people about one of the progressive dinners that he claims is one of my 'greatest culinary achievements'. I was in charge of the canapés, but as usual I was running late. With no time on my hands I turned up late to my own apartment with a couple of packets of Samboy potato chips. John has never let me live it down.

John's got quite a few stories on me from those days. There was one incident in particular that he says 'sums me up to a T.' John and I went out for dinner at one of the local restaurants in Portsea. We were sitting there, chatting away and enjoying the night, when John accidentally tipped his wine glass. Although he just managed to catch the glass by the stem it was too late, and most of the red wine emptied all up the front of the white collared shirt I was wearing. He apologised profusely, but I told him 'no stress mate', and mopped myself up. A little while later we were joined by some of the others who had been working all night at Delgany, including Darren. According to John, Darren took one look at me, saw the huge red wine stain all over the white shirt and said 'Luke, that's my brand new shirt!'

While Delgany was a hard slog and we all lived in fear of Hermann, the irony now is every one of his protégés love him. We all love what he instilled in us: the commitment it takes, the work ethic. There are few people in this industry who I respect more than Hermann Schneider.

As I mentioned, it was during my time at Delgany that Hermann had given me a major compliment for the very first time, and it had finally made me proud to be a chef. And perhaps, for the first time in my life, I was beginning to believe in myself.

There were a lot of great times down in Portsea, and more importantly, as I neared the end of my apprenticeship it was dawning on me that I had the ability to carve out a career as a chef. But just as life was on the up, I had bad news from home. Dad was unwell, and it was very serious.

7

TRAGEDY STRIKES

Dad died in the winter of 1989. It was devastating for our family. I'd turned 19 that May and was nearing the end of my apprenticeship. It felt like I was finally becoming my own man, but looking back now, I was still just a young kid in many ways. I'm not sure I was really able to comprehend what was going on, and it took me a bit to fully grasp the magnitude of it all.

Dad had a disease known as aplastic anaemia. He was diagnosed with leukaemia as a child, and I think it might have been connected, but I'm only a chef, I couldn't be sure. In all honesty, at the time of his illness I didn't really think about his illness or what it was, I just wanted Dad to be okay.

Aplastic anaemia is essentially a god-awful kind of blood cancer. It's a complicated condition where the bone marrow fails

TRAGEDY STRIKES

to produce enough new cells to replenish blood cells. Essentially it means that those with the disease have a lower count of all three types of blood cells: white, red and platelets. The platelets only last five or six days, so the bone marrow needs to produce them regularly. That was the problem: Dad's bone marrow just couldn't produce them and basically it meant his immune system was shot, his heart was enlarged, and his body no longer had the ability to fight off infection. Essentially he was stuffed.

It was only a matter of six months from the time Dad was diagnosed to the time he passed away. He really deteriorated quite rapidly. I was living down in Portsea working at Delgany during most of Dad's illness, so I was kind of separated from my family in the sense that I didn't see his day-to-day degeneration.

The last month was pretty intense. I was heading up to Melbourne as regularly as I could. Because his condition was so rare, the doctors really didn't know how to treat it. At one stage they put him on horse serum, but that didn't seem to work. The doctors suggested a machine that could use the blood of our family members and take out the platelets, and if they were compatible they could give Dad blood transfusions. Because Dad couldn't produce a sufficient amount of platelets it seemed like a real solution.

I asked Mum about that time and she remembers it much better than me. 'Towards the end his platelets would drop and he needed blood transfusions regularly. You boys had to be tested to see if your blood platelets could be used. We have a laugh now because Tim, who's always been extremely fit, was bragging that his healthy blood would be perfect, and he'd carry on saying he'd have the best platelets because he's a fitness fanatic. We had to laugh about it because when he was tested his platelets weren't compatible at all.'

I remember in the early days we'd go into the hospital and donate blood without even thinking about it, like it was just another day. When someone is close to you, you just get on your bike and pedal hard, you just get on with it and you do what you can to help them. You don't think about it, you just do it.

Fortunately my platelets were a match and they were produced at a high level too. I'm not sure why, perhaps it's because I was the youngest, and being only 19 I was probably jam-packed full of testosterone too. They seemed to be working, that's all that mattered. I remember Mum ringing to tell me that the doctor had asked to get me back in because I had great platelets and it was giving Dad a bit of a lift. For two or three days following a blood transfusion Dad really perked up and had a real colour in him, it was really nice to see him more sprightly. Sadly though, the blood transfusions only helped for a little while, and really they were just delaying the inevitable.

Dad died on Friday 30 June at about 3:20pm. As a bank manager, Dad was always on top of the books and figures, so now we look back at it with a warm grin because it's as if he got to the end of the financial year, was satisfied he had balanced the books and he'd done his job, and then he signed off.

Dad died on the Friday and the funeral was on the following Tuesday. I took the rest of the week off and some of the boys and I stayed with Mum in Forrest Hill. As you'd imagine, she was completely distraught. We all were. It doesn't matter how much you prepare yourself, it's very, very soul destroying. When someone so close to you passes away I don't think you get a chance to think of what their influence was in your life. Time stands still and you kind of brush that all under the rug, because your heart is so heavy from dealing with the shock of it all. But from that moment on they are always in your

TRAGEDY STRIKES

mind. These moments make you realise our frailties and how fleeting life can be. There are really only a few things that are important in our entire lifetimes.

One thing I'm thankful for is that the entire family was together in the room when Dad passed.

The week after Dad's funeral I made my way back to Portsea and went straight back to work, but I was very unmotivated. I was moping around and I couldn't get up for work in the mornings. I just worked in the kitchen and did my hours, but my heart wasn't in it.

Hermann had met my dad a few times and I think they had a mutual admiration and respect for each other. They shared a kind of discipline and an attitude that hard work made the man. The week after my dad died we had a pretty busy night service at Delgany. I just couldn't pull it together and I was really letting the team down, so Hermann pulled me into his office. I just broke down and started crying. It was finally all just hitting home that my dad was gone forever. Hermann, to his credit, offered some kind words that I'll never forget.

'Your behaviour and the way you are putting your tail between your legs, that's not what your dad would want you to do. He would really want you to succeed. Your dad was a great man, he would want you to make him proud.'

He paused for a minute and put his hand on my shoulder, then said, 'Just look at your brother, and look how well your brother is doing as a chef and what he has achieved.'

That moment was all a blur to me, but Hermann tells me he's never forgotten my reply. 'You looked me straight in the eye and said "Well Mr Schneider, I'm going to be better than him!".'

That was a real tough time for me, but almost four years earlier I'd promised my dad that if I left school I had to complete my trade qualifications under Hermann Schneider. Unfortunately Dad never saw me finish my apprenticeship, but I certainly wasn't going to let him down.

8

THE PHONE CALL

About four months after Dad's passing I finally completed my apprenticeship. It was a monumental achievement. I'd done it. Four fucking years of hard slog under Hermann's watchful eye had finally paid off. Little did I know at the time, that I had a hell of a lot to learn yet.

Gaining my apprenticeship papers proved once and for all that if I put my mind to something, no matter how big or small, I could do it. It was recognition for all the hard work, and to celebrate we held one hell of a party, most of which I can't remember, but I'm told it was very good.

I was still at Delgany under Hermann Schneider, and after all of my years slaving away in the kitchen I felt like I needed a bit of breathing space. I was still dealing with the loss of Dad at that stage, and since

I'd achieved my qualifications I took the opportunity to take some leave, clear my head and work out where the hell my career would lead me.

My brother Matt had been to Bali and had an absolute blast. The food, the good times, the weather, and it was so cheap as well. I asked Hermann for two weeks' annual leave and booked a flight to Bali. I grabbed my backpack and headed overseas for the very first time in my life.

It was late in the year and summer was in full swing. I remember stepping off the plane in Bali and being bowled over by an intensely muggy heat, but boy I was grinning from ear to bloody ear. I took a deep breath and then leaped into the unknown. I was on my own, with no rules, no inhibitions and really, for ten whole days the world, or Bali at least, was my oyster.

First off I made my way to Kuta, just like every other bloody Aussie, and found a cheap backpackers my brother Matt had recommended: Sri Ratu Bungalows. I dropped off my bag and walked through the streets to get a taste of things to come.

The streets were chaos: a montage of sounds, sights and smells, and it was intoxicating. It wasn't long before I was amongst the bevy of street markets sampling the array of hawker food on offer. Boy, my adversity to spicy food got a real workout, I can tell you. I've always had a sensitive stomach, and the uncertainty of what I was actually eating certainly put it to the test. From saté skewers to gado gado (a vegetable salad) and bakso (a meatball soup) or even the rujak, where tropical fruits swim in a tamarind and chilli sauce, the food was electric. With an adventurous spirit I reckon I handled it pretty well, but these days I'd be a bit more mindful of what I sampled, that's for sure.

THE PHONE CALL

Bali was where I experienced my first taste of tequila. It was far more than a taste. The morning after I was probably about as violently ill as you can get. I swore I'd never drink tequila again.

I rented a scooter and joined the throng of madmen hooning around the streets, weaving between pedestrians at a million miles an hour. I can't believe there aren't more accidents really, it was wild!

One day I ventured up into the mountains with a group of travellers I'd met. We picked vanilla beans, lychees and rambutans from the trees. The flavours and aromas were a revelation: so fresh, so simple and so memorable. I'd never experienced anything like it. From what I knew, all the produce arrived at the back door of the kitchen, packaged neatly and labelled. Getting out there and experiencing fresh food straight from the land made me think about food, and the manner in which we consume it, completely differently.

I had the time of my life in Bali. It was a real eye-opener, and I realised there was a whole world out there waiting. Perhaps it was time to branch out, leave the nest and go explore it. But what was I going to do?

French chef Michel Roux was a hero of mine. His restaurant, The Waterside Inn, on the banks of the Thames in Bray, England, was one of the few restaurants in the world with three Michelin stars. In fact, it still is. 30-odd years as a three-star Michelin restaurant: unbelievable. The man is incredible. Michel and his brother Albert had released a book called *The Roux Brothers on Patisserie* and Michel had toured Australia to promote it. I fucking loved it. It was the most amazing book I'd ever seen. I read it from cover to cover and tried to cook practically everything inside it. It sparked a real enthusiasm and passion for food that I'd probably not experienced before.

Hermann and Mr Roux were good friends, so he had been to Two Faces in South Yarra before, and while on his book tour he ventured down to Portsea for dinner at Delgany. I didn't meet him that night, but I remember the kitchen brigade was very keen to impress. When you talk of culinary kings, of culinary icons, of food heroes, there are few, if any, that come close to Mr Roux.

If I was up for a challenge, why not aim high and see if I could get a gig in the kitchen of one of the best restaurants in the world—The Waterside Inn? I had nothing to lose, surely.

I got back from Bali and asked Hermann if he could help me get in contact with Mr Roux at The Waterside Inn. Hermann, to his credit, was right behind me 100 per cent. He'd got five years out of me, which was almost a record for a chef under his guidance.

Hermann warned me that it's not so easy to just ask for a job and get one. At that stage Mr Roux was a global phenomenon, and the holder of three Michelin stars too. Hermann told me that Mr Roux would have apprentices and chefs from all over the world asking to come and work for him and be mentored by him. 'But by all means you should try,' he said.

I wrote a letter to Mr Roux saying that I'd be coming over to London in a few months' time and I wanted to work at The Waterside Inn. I explained my training under Hermann Schneider, and how hard I was willing to work if he'd give me a chance. Hermann even helped me with the letter and let me use the Two Faces Delgany letterhead to get Mr Roux' attention.

Two weeks later I received a letter from Mr Roux. It basically said 'Thank you for your letter, but we have no positions available within that time frame, it's a two-year waiting list.'

I was gutted. In my mind I already had the whole trip worked

THE PHONE CALL

out. I'd decided I'd be going to London. I had the money saved, the mindset locked in and to be knocked back just hit me for six.

I was a bit down in the dumps so I decided to use my days off to go and visit Mum back at the family home in Forrest Hill. After a long chat with Mum about how disappointed I was about it, I got so worked up I thought fuck it, I'll ring him. I'll ring Mr Roux and ask him if I can come and work for him. I had no idea what I was going to say, but I picked up the phone and rang The Waterside Inn.

It was late at night in Australia, which made it mid-morning in the UK. They'd be in the throes of preparing for the lunch service.

A manager answered the phone and I asked if I could be transferred to the kitchen because I wanted to speak to the chef, Mr Roux. I couldn't believe it, they just transferred me through.

A chef answered, and said 'Kitchen'.

I nervously replied 'Can I speak to Mr Roux, please?'

'Speaking,' replied the voice.

I couldn't believe it. It was the man himself.

I stuttered and stammered and finally said, 'My name is Luke Mangan, I'm calling from Australia. I work for Hermann Schneider, I wrote you a letter ...'

'I got your letter,' he interrupted, 'and my response said there's a two-year waiting list, did it not?'

'It did,' I said. 'But I really want to work for you, Mr Roux, and I'm coming over anyway in a few weeks.'

He said 'I'm sorry Luke, but it's a two-year waiting list, best of luck.'

My heart sank. I panicked because the dream was practically over. Without even thinking, I said, 'What if I work a month without pay, and if I'm any good you can give me a job, and if I'm not I'm out the door?'

He said 'Okay Luke, see you in a few weeks.'

We agreed that he'd give me laundry, accommodation and I could eat staff meals every day.

I got off the phone and jumped about two metres in the air. What the hell was I thinking? A month without pay in London? But what an opportunity!

Hermann and John Lepp were delighted for me. Hermann warned me that it'd be no cup of tea. He said 'You think you worked hard for me Luke, don't forget you are going to one of the best restaurants in the world. It's not going to be easy.'

I was pretty nervous about the whole thing. I had a long chat with John Lepp about what to expect in that sort of kitchen. Would Mr Roux be scarier than Hermann? Was that at all possible? I wasn't even sure if I could afford to go there and support myself in London with no pay. Really, it was madness. I'd never even been to England. Although board and laundry were taken care of I'd essentially be working for free.

John told me not to worry about it. 'Just go there and prove to them you are worth a job and you can cut it,' he said. 'If you do that, if you believe in yourself and work hard, you'll get a job in no time at all.'

I grabbed my backpack and off I went. London beckoned.

9

THE WATERSIDE INN

I touched down in England at the beginning of May, 1990. I had a few days up my sleeve so I found myself a backpackers in London, then wandered aimlessly around the tourist traps until it was time to head down to Bray, where I'd get a start at The Waterside Inn.

I arrived at the restaurant at about 4pm on 5 May. I only remember the exact date because it was the day before my 21st birthday.

I was more nervous than I'd ever been in my life. The reality was I didn't even have a job there. I had to prove myself first, and I wasn't sure if I had enough skills to do that. Hermann and John had given me a solid grounding, but was it enough for The Waterside Inn? At least I had my foot in the door, so it was a good start. In truth, maybe the only person stopping me from getting a job was myself.

Someone showed me upstairs and put me in a tiny room that I'd be sharing with a crazy French guy. This is what I'd call home: a bed, a side table and a wardrobe, plus a roommate who spoke little or no English.

The daily ritual of staff meals occurred at 5pm on the dot. So it wasn't long after I arrived before the staff meal was ready. It was like your first day at school. You don't know anyone, you feel out of place and really awkward. No one seemed particularly interested in me, so I just grabbed a plate, filled it with food and looked for somewhere to plonk myself down.

All the chefs were sitting on one side of the room shovelling food into their mouths, while the waiters were sitting together on the other side. No one spoke to me and I didn't say anything to anyone either. It was awful. All the waiters were speaking in French, so I had no idea what they were talking about, and most of the chefs were French too. I still can't speak anything other than 'Kitchen French'.

There was a table with one chair on its own in the corner of the room, so I made a beeline for it and nervously sat, eating as quickly as I could. I offloaded my plate to the kitchen porter and went back upstairs to my room. I was lying on my bed thinking *what the hell am I doing here?* I felt completely unwelcome and intimidated. It was tough under Hermann, but was this going to me my worst fucking nightmare?

The night service started downstairs at 6pm. My bed was directly above the kitchen and I could hear everything that was going on. All the orders were announced over a microphone through speakers because the kitchen was so large, and it was almost like being at a train station, except everything was in French. I had no idea what they were saying.

I could hear the rumbling of deep voices, randomly overwhelmed by the voice over the PA, coupled with the typical clanging and crashing sounds of a commercial kitchen in full swing. It made me even more nervous about my start the following day. So I grabbed my copies of *The Roux Brothers on Patisserie* and *New Classic Cuisine*, and tried to memorise as much as I could.

The nerves were getting the better of me. At about 7pm I went for a walk. The village of Bray is quite small so it doesn't take long to walk around it. I kept thinking of how many fuck-ups I'd make in the morning and wondered if I was going to blow my opportunity. I was so nervous that I threw up in someone's front garden. I wiped my mouth, shook my head and thought: *What the fuck is going on? Pull it together, Mangan!*

I decided to go back and try to sleep. But not even Sleeping Beauty could sleep in a bed directly above a commercial kitchen in the middle of service. I was awake all night.

I had to be downstairs ready for work by 7am, but, eager to get cracking, I was down there at 6:30am on the dot. The head chef, Mark Dodson, didn't get in until 7:30am so a chef de partie gave me a tour of the kitchen before Mark arrived and assigned me to the fish butchery section.

My first shift at The Waterside Inn, on my 21st birthday mind you, went from 7am until 1am. I didn't tell anyone it was my birthday, and no one knew. No one ever knew.

The next morning an English guy named Marcus Ashenford started in the kitchen. He's got a cracking one-Michelin-star restaurant in the Cotswold town of Winchcombe now, named No.5 North Street.

We hit it off immediately and became great mates. Gus, as I called him, landed the canape section. Poor bastard; it was probably the hardest section at The Waterside Inn. He was in charge of three canapés and an amuse bouche per guest, plus he would do all the salads as well. Lunch and dinner, that's a lot of fucking canapés.

Aged 7 months.
Nice outfit, thanks mum!

Looking pretty happy about my hair do! Aged 2.

School photo. Gee I must have been about 10 or 11. I reckon just before I became a constant truant!

Hmm, just not the sort of grades parents dream of their kids achieving! I was hopeless at school!

Voila! My first attempt at souffles at age 15.

Looking sharp for a job interview at Two Faces!

Off to conquer the world (in London). Can't believe that backpack held all my belongings for three years!

Argh! The breakfast shift in the kitchen at Two Faces, Delgany in 1989

A serious hat for a serious chef! In the kitchen of The Waterside Inn.

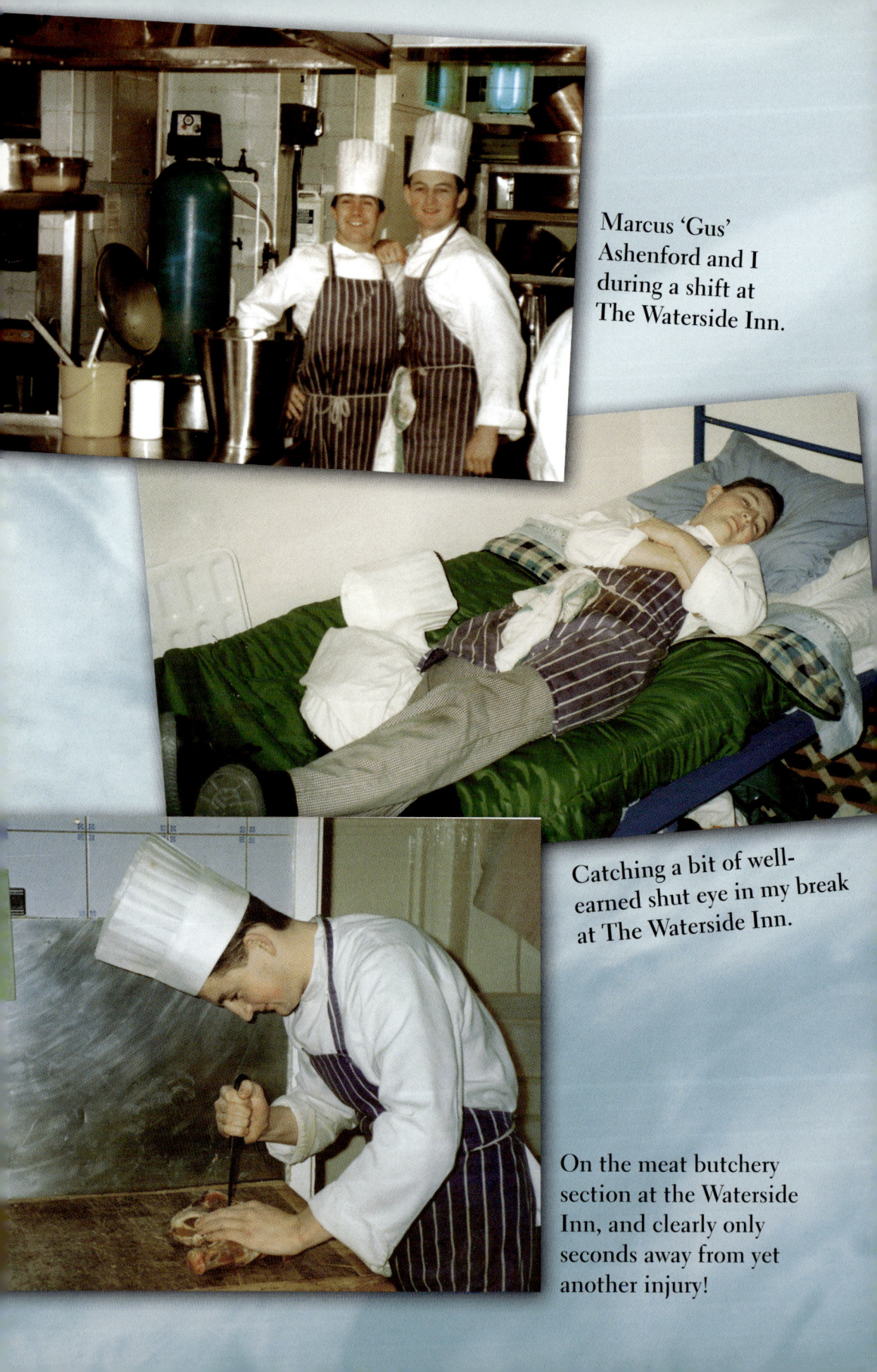

Marcus 'Gus' Ashenford and I during a shift at The Waterside Inn.

Catching a bit of well-earned shut eye in my break at The Waterside Inn.

On the meat butchery section at the Waterside Inn, and clearly only seconds away from yet another injury!

The huge kitchen brigade at The Waterside Inn. My mate Gus is on the left back row, I'm third from the left back row and Mr Roux is second from left front row.

Marcus 'Gus' Ashenford and I kick'n back for a brew after another long shift at The Waterside Inn.

With my great mate David Rayner outside The Palace. Boy we had a few pints there!

My signature dish liquorice parfait, created in the kitchen at CBD after a lot of trial and error!

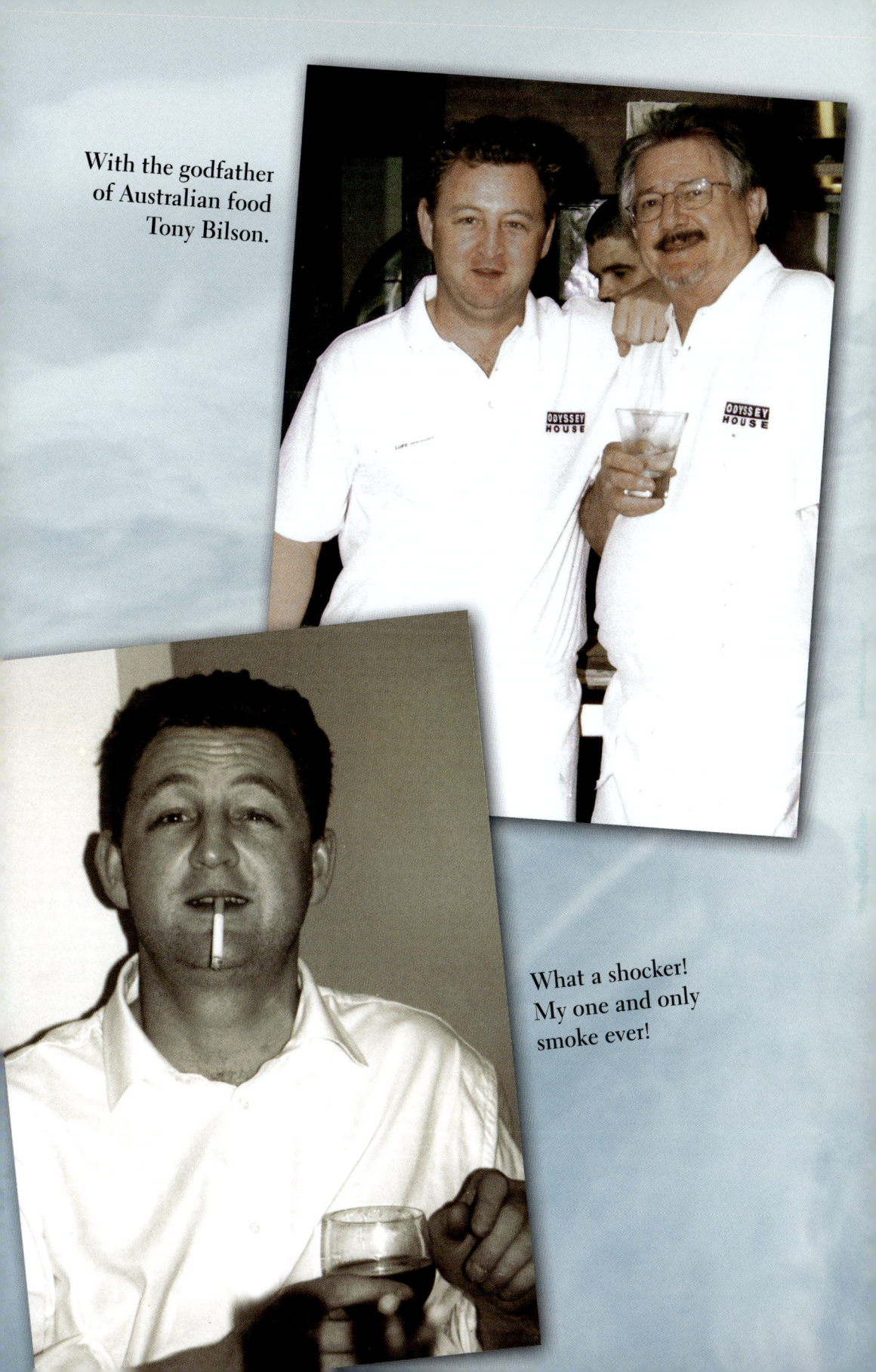

With the godfather of Australian food Tony Bilson.

What a shocker! My one and only smoke ever!

Giving Tetsuya Wakuda moral support while he cooks at his place during the 90s.

If I had landed that section I don't think I would have lasted. Not a chance. Gus was a machine, I don't know how he did it. Thankfully I got fish butchery. I wasn't that great at that either, but it wasn't as fiddly as most of the other sections and although the hours were long, the pressure wasn't on me as much. But you still couldn't let the team down.

Fish butchery was smelly, slimy and wet, and that was on a good day. I'd be dealing with all sorts of species: sea bass, turbot, dory, lobster, scampi, prawns, you name it. You'd get your fish, gut it, fillet it, skin it and have it ready for service. It was messy hard yakka, and not as delicate as other sections because you aren't actually in the kitchen doing service. Boy I stank. You think it smells down at the fish markets, try cutting up fish all day, every day.

There was one special fish that was a nightmare to do. We'd get a whole turbot in and it was a big turbot too. I'd prepare them into portions called 'tranche'. You take your turbot and make an incision at the end of the tail, then with a sharp knife, cut around where the fin ends and the meat starts. This is to remove the fins. Then you have to skin it. That was a real nightmare, I can tell you right now, skinning a turbot is not much fun at all. You have to use a towel and be very, very careful not to leave a single bit of skin on it. If I buggered it up, I'd have to grab another one and start again; there was no room for error in a three-Michelin-star restaurant. After all of this work on the turbot, you cut its head off with the shears, gut it, and then cut it into tranches—basically two fillets.

We also had a dish called *truit au bleu*, which was trout cooked in a white wine sauce. That was my worst nightmare. We had the trout live in a tank, so I would have to get the live fish from the tank and kill it to order. In those days we basically bashed it on the back of the head. Sounds scary, but that's how we killed it. Then I had to gut it, trim it up and pass it on to the fish cook, all done a la carte.

We also had a stunning lobster dish: lobster medallions with a white port sauce and ginger. So guess who had to kill the lobsters to order?

I'd done a little bit of meat and fish butchery at Two Faces but nothing had prepared me for this. The guy I took over from on fish butchery would rock in at 8am and be done by 6pm, whereas I'd be there at 6:30am and still be there at 9:30–10pm. I was slow, I was always in the shit and I just couldn't do it as quickly as these guys, at the quality required.

Mr Roux was different to Hermann: he wouldn't bollock you. He'd certainly raise his voice if you stuffed up, but Mr Roux always moved on straight afterwards. And just like John Lepp at Two Faces, The Waterside Inn head chef Mark Dodson was great, a real inspiration and a patient teacher too.

There was a certain level of respect at The Waterside Inn, like a hierarchy. It was intense, but it was never abusive. If you fucked up, you had to stay until you finished it properly. You might be there until three in the morning. It didn't matter, as long as you had everything ready for the next day's service.

The end of my first month came up, and Mr Roux, Mark and I sat down to discuss whether there was a paid job for me at The Waterside Inn. I sat there nervously. Mark didn't say anything; Mr Roux did all the talking.

He was short and sweet about it, he said, 'Luke, you've been here a month, you've worked really hard, so we'd like to offer you a job.'

What a fucking relief, and boy I needed the money.

But though I obviously needed to make a living, I never went to The Waterside Inn for money. If you are good at what you do and you're committed to it, then the money will come. A lot of apprentices come into the industry for money and fame; they come into it for the wrong reasons. They don't realise how hard the work is. It's fucking hard, and forget *Masterchef*. As much as it has raised the interest in food, contestants will never know how hard it is to do an apprenticeship until they get into a commercial kitchen and peel spuds for a whole day, for a whole year.

So I got 90 pounds net income, and they took 25 quid a week for board. I worked a 60 to 70 hour week and got one day off. Monday was my day to do all my washing, go to the pub, get pissed and be in bed by 9pm so I could get up early Tuesday and work the whole week again. That routine was like clockwork for the first year.

A couple of chefs who've made their mark on the Australian and international restaurant industry were working in the kitchen when I arrived at The Waterside Inn: Michael Lambie, known for Taxi Dining Room in Melbourne and Donovan Cooke at the Crown complex with The Atlantic. Michael was chef de partie fish and Donovan was chef de partie meat.

They called me Oz at The Waterside Inn. Some called me Skippy. You know some of the chefs there were complete pricks to me. You have to find your place in the pecking order in a place like that, and I wasn't that far from the bottom. I was barely above the kitchen porters. So I just put my head down and worked hard. Yes chef, no chef, three bags full chef all over again.

Gus and I were the new guys on the block and we had to earn our stripes in the eyes of the brigade before they'd consider showing us any sort of respect. It's the same in any serious kitchen. The attitude towards the 'new chefs' was 'if they are still here in six months then maybe we'll talk to them.'

It was my first winter in London, and it was pretty tough. Sure, Melbourne gets pretty cold, but not like this. Plus all I had was a bloody sleeping bag, and there's only so much clothing you can fit into a backpack, so I was freezing. But that's all part of the experience. You don't have the opportunities in Australia, like you do in England, to duck over to France, Spain and Italy and try different cuisines. Cheffing is the most transferable job there is. Chefs have a ticket to the world and you're mad if you don't take advantage of that.

I was on fish butchery for six months before Mr Roux moved me to meat butchery: a promotion to commis chef. I was just as bad on meat butchery as I was on fish. It took me forever to get my work done. The fish were often killed to order, but a lot of the meat had to be butchered before service. It was okay not to be there during service, but you had to be precise with everything you did.

Donovan Cooke was on meat, so I was essentially butchering meat for him to cook. I guess he kind of took me under his wing, and I think he came to the realisation 'maybe this kid can cut it in this kitchen.'

There were dishes that I've never forgotten, and the basic butchery behind them was integral to the dish's success. Mr Roux's saddle of lamb was beautiful. We'd bone out the saddle, make a beautiful mint farce for the stuffing, roll it, roast it and serve it with petite veg and a mint hollandaise. Delicious: really simple but really, really good. We also had a rabbit dish with glazed chestnuts. We used to make a crouton in the shape of a rabbit and sit it on the top of the plate. Thinking back now, it sounds very old-fashioned!

I learned a lot doing meat butchery, and I have a lot of battle scars to prove it. Amazingly, I'd lasted about six months of fish butchery without an injury. However, in my first week on meat butchery, I was boning out a saddle of lamb when the knife slipped. It went deep into the side of my fucking thumb and you could see the bone. I was off to the hospital, and five or six stitches later I was back in the kitchen to finish the day's prep. I was pretty embarrassed. You're meant to know what you are doing, or at least make it look like you do!

Of course, I soon learned that happened quite a bit to every chef in the meat butchery section. It was part and parcel of the gig. Everyone had a battle scar or two.

It wasn't the worst injury I'd experience at The Waterside Inn. A few months later I was walking through the kitchen when I slipped and did some serious damage. In a section of the kitchen the benches were arranged in an L shape, and it meant there was only one way through to the prep kitchen. We used to store the stockpot bubbling away around the corner of the L and on the odd occasion it would leak. As I was turning the corner I slipped, and flexed my arm out to catch myself from falling. Unfortunately I missed the bench top and my whole arm went into the boiling stockpot. I pulled it out immediately and there was skin coming off my arm everywhere. I freaked out and the chefs quickly got it under cold water, and then I was off to the hospital again. I got wrapped up and went back to work. No excuses in those days, I was one-armed but I had work to do. What else was I going to do anyway? Get back to work chef. Yes chef.

After six months of meat butchery I was promoted to demi chef. It was a huge move for a young chef, especially after just 12 months in the kitchen. It meant I had moved up to the sauce section, a position I'd hold for the last 12 months at The Waterside Inn.

For a 22-year-old to be working on the meat, sauce and garnish section of a three-star Michelin restaurant, it's the sort of grounding you could only dream of.

10

KP AND ROWLEY LEIGH

I sent a letter to Swiss chef Fredy Girardet asking if there was any chance I could get a job cooking at his restaurant Girardet in Crissier, Switzerland. He was another culinary king, and one of the 'godfathers of French cooking'—just like Mr Roux.

There was a bit of mystique about him, because many critics had labelled him the greatest chef in the world, and his restaurant the best in the world. But people knew little about him. I wanted to find out for myself.

I'd spent two years in the kitchen of The Waterside Inn. It was not a crash course in the art of cooking, it was a definitive exposure to the way things should be, or perhaps how things could be done if you dared to aim high enough.

I hadn't really done my time there at Waterside; some of the guys had been there five to 10 years. Although there was a lot more I could have learned, I felt it was enough for me and I was keen for a new challenge.

About two weeks later I received a letter in the post from Mr Girardet. It read 'Mr Mangan,'... I stopped reading. The whole blasted letter was in French! It was quite a long letter and I had no idea if I'd got the job or if he told me to go stick it!

By this time I was staying in staff accommodation off premises, and although it was my day off I had to know what this letter said, so I made my way to work hoping to catch a French waiter or chef and have them translate it for me.

'He says no,' was the response of one of the French chefs.

He said no? But it was a whole page?

So I said, 'what does he say, what are the reasons?'

'He says no because of your visa, he doesn't want to sponsor you, and he has no places as well.'

What a letdown. Who writes that much for a rejection letter!

That was disappointing, but my mind was made up, I needed a change.

My mate from the Sorrento days, Darren (Daggy) Barnett, was in the UK at that time and he was working at a restaurant in London that was getting huge raps in the press. It was being labelled a leader of 'modern British cookery'.

It was Kensington Place, which we called KP, and it was owned by a Roux protégé, Rowley Leigh. He'd opened it in 1987 with front of house gurus Nick Smallwood, Simon Slater and Thirsty Edwards. It had won *The Times* Restaurant of the Year and was on everyone's lips. In its simplest form it was a 200-seat brasserie. Rowley attempted to take all the great parts of fine dining, strip it back and present it in a more casual environment without losing its sheen.

Rowley had been a chef at Le Gavroche, the Roux brothers' pastry laboratory, as well as working as a buyer for them. So he was classically trained, but he yearned for a restaurant where the dining experience was free of that stiff pretentiousness, while the clever techniques in the kitchen would deliver simple combinations that smacked of full flavours. KP hit the nail on the head.

I caught up with Daggy for a drink one afternoon in London and he told me that Rowley was looking for more chefs because they'd renovated the restaurant. The larger size dining room would require more staff to man it and feed the extra punters. It sounded really exciting so I rang Rowley. He knew what happened in a Roux kitchen and he was eager to give me a go.

I was given the title of chef de partie and I set up some temporary accommodation at The Palace. It was a big pub with backpacker accommodation attached to it. I shared a room with eight others including an Irish guy named Anthony, who I'd eventually get share accommodation with about six months later.

KP was a big change for me. I went from formal French dining to a brasserie that seated about 200, and it took a little while for me to get settled.

Rowley Leigh's a very intellectual man. He has a Bachelor of Arts degree, he's a writer and accomplished chef. He would always talk with big sentences and big words that I didn't even know the meaning of half the time. He spoke very quickly and sounded way more intelligent than me.

Rowley's demeanour was different to both Hermann and Mr Roux. Although he demanded attention to detail and the best from all his employees, he was fun to work with and often displayed a witty and irreverent sense of humour, which at times could take the edge off the stress of a busy night.

KP was a lot easier than The Waterside Inn because it was a brasserie, but that didn't diminish the high standards required. I was probably a bit too cocky too because I'd just come out of The Waterside Inn, I thought I was the fucking king of the castle. As a result, I rubbed some chefs up the wrong way. The sous chefs hated me, but I got on well with Rowley, and the sous chefs hated that as well. The sous chefs would often try to stitch me up all the time by giving me the specials of the day at 5:55pm just before we opened, without any prior warning. I had no idea what the specials were, let alone how to make them.

I'd hate to think that sort of behaviour would go on in any of my kitchens. I don't understand what the point of doing that was. At the end of the day you are just fucking up the customer because you are rushing everything. They were the chefs running the show at the time and I guess they wanted to make sure they had the power.

There were several staff members who started the same day as me, including an English chef named David Rayner. He was hired as a junior sous chef. Since David and I were the new chefs on the block we sort of teamed up. David and I just decided to work hard. I'd be first one in and often last one to leave. The hierarchy in the kitchen those days was very structured and much like what I experienced under Hermann, but on a larger scale. David and I bonded together at first because no one else wanted to talk to us.

We spent quite a bit of time working together and working opposite each other too. I would do the stoves, grill or the fish section and David might do the vegetables or larder, and that really helped to create a bond and trust between us.

KP AND ROWLEY LEIGH

We worked in unison, and he would need parts of my dish or I would need parts of his, so there was a lot of calling to one another and relying on one another in the kitchen during service.

We weren't really like a lot of the others in the kitchen. We didn't have the attitude that they had. We just wanted to come in to work, do our jobs, work hard, cook well and not get caught up in all the bullshit, the anger, the bitterness and selfishness that can perpetuate in those sort of kitchens because of that strong sense of order and ranking. We just got on with it and did our job and I think Rowley really liked that about us.

In the kitchen Rowley was a master with game meat. I learned a lot about grouse, partridge, snipe, quail, you name it. When I was on butchery at The Waterside Inn I used to have to pluck the whole birds, and it ain't easy, but I'm glad I learned it before KP.

We'd get in twelve fresh ducks. Rowley would have arranged for someone to shoot them, so they'd be as fresh as you could get. They'd come in on the feather and you'd spend all day plucking these damn ducks. You have no idea how hard it is to pluck a duck, let alone twelve. Rowley did a stunning grouse with a traditional bread sauce too. Once the food hit the plate it was just all about simple, honest, full flavours. We'd do things like a great steak, chips and a cracking bernaise. It was bistro food, classic but in a modern light.

KP was all about the produce. Rowley was a big influence in that regard. The nice thing was that I had that disciplined classical training under Hermann, and then an even more defined and precise training under Mr Roux at The Waterside Inn. You still had that at KP but Rowley's approach was a little more modern and fresh. Combining the discipline of the Waterside and Rowley's approach to food was a great basis to creating my own food.

Just like all my other jobs I was doing 60 to 70 hours a week. It never felt like too much, it was just the nature of the beast.

One afternoon while cooking away at KP I felt like I had something in my right eye. My vision was blurred, and no matter how many times I tried to wash it out it remained really blurry. It was as annoying as hell but I just got on with work and assumed soon enough it would get better. Eyes generally have a clever natural way of weeping out any foreign objects.

The next morning I woke up and it wasn't any better. I realised that wasn't probably a good thing, so I took off to the doctor, who ushered me off to an eye specialist in London. They did a whole bunch of tests and came to the conclusion that I had toxoplasmosis in the back of my right eye. For some people it is quite common, and you can even get it on your skin apparently.

The most common way of getting it is from cats. We never had a cat growing up, and to be honest I've never been the biggest fan of cats anyway. Another way of getting it is by handling raw meat. This seemed a lot more likely. Had all the meat butchery I had endured through my career thus far attributed to getting toxoplasmosis in my right eye? I'll never know, but it did some serious damage.

I have lost the vision in the top part of my right eye. Sound confusing? You should see it through my eyes. It's basically eaten away the top half of my vision.

As a kid, I was cross-eyed. I had a turned eye, well both of them turned at different stages. That's why I wore those huge Coke bottle glasses. My eyes were shithouse. I ended up having three different operations on them. First they operated on my right eye, then my left one turned and they operated on that as well. So I wore eye patches a fair bit too—no wonder I got picked on as a kid. I also had an allergic reaction to the anesthetic in the last operation, which caused a lot of problems.

So maybe I was a bit more susceptible to toxoplasmosis than others. All I know is it's pretty damn annoying, but it could be worse, I could have no sight at all. I guess in some ways I have gotten used to it, you have to. I've seen a mountain of eye specialists all over the world to try and sort it out, but all of them have told me that with the toxoplasmosis, I'm always going to be like this. It's irreparable damage. Worse still, it could reactivate and I could lose more vision, or all of it. Fingers crossed, and until that moment, carpe diem baby, I'll seize the day!

At this stage, it had been a few years since Dad had died. Mum and Dad had always wanted to come over to the UK, especially Ireland where Dad's family were from. So to give Mum a bit of a lift, all seven of us kids had agreed to chip in and buy her a trip to the UK. My brother Michael and I were both working there at the time and agreed to show Mum a good time.

Mum always reminds me of the moment I met her at the airport. I was a pretty disorganised kid in those days, and some things never change. I knew Mum was coming, but I kind of flew by the seat of my pants the morning she landed.

When she walked out of Customs I had literally just arrived, and was standing there with an Indian guy. Mum thought he must be a friend of mine. She was pretty confused and shocked when I introduced him to her as our taxi driver. I just thought since I'd got the taxi there and I was late, there would be no point getting in the taxi line for 20 minutes when we left. Ten quid and a bit of friendly chat solved that problem.

So we got into the taxi and started driving. It was late at night and the best plan was to stay in London before heading to my place. Mum asked where we were going to stay the night. I had nothing.

'I don't know,' I said.

She went off at me! 'What do you mean you don't know? I've flown for 24 hours, I've just arrived, I'm tired and you don't know where we are staying?'

'The taxi driver will know somewhere for us stay, won't you mate?' I asked awkwardly.

So he drove us to a place he thought would suit. It didn't look too bad but Mum wanted to have a look around the place first before agreeing to stay the night. They took her into the bathroom, and she turned to me and said, 'well I'm not staying here unless the shower is cleaned.'

Mothers! I'm sure she was thinking the opposite: *Sons!*

They cleaned the shower and we ended up staying. We made our way to my place in the morning. At this stage I'd left The Palace and moved into my own small room in a big old mansion. It must have had about seven or eight rooms. My room was upstairs and about the size of a bloody shoebox: just enough room for a single bed, a chair and a bag. I even had to put a 20 pence coin into a slot just to use the heater and keep warm. It was crazy, but it suited because I wasn't there much.

What I didn't realise until about a year later was that some of the rooms downstairs housed 'ladies of the night', and essentially half the house was used as a bloody brothel! The rest of the rooms were rented out to working travellers like me. It was one of those big old-fashioned grand London homes and they were so discreet, you'd never know it was happening. Well I certainly never knew, but then again I was never there, and when I was there I'd be stumbling home drunk, or I'd be in a rush to leave because I was late for work. When you live in a shoebox, there's not much incentive to 'stay in for the night'.

When Mum came over I had to host her in this tiny room. She slept in the bed and I slept on the floor in a sleeping bag. So although I was oblivious to the fact, I was hosting my mother, who'd flown across the world, in a bloody brothel. What was I thinking?

I sometimes wonder if she knew. Well, she will now.

I'd taken a week off work and we had an absolute ball touring London, but the highlight for the three of us was the trip to Ireland. Some of my dad's side of the family are originally from Cork so the three of us made our way there just in time for an annual music festival in the town centre. There was lovely Irish music on the streets and buskers everywhere. Mum even got carried away and started dancing on the street. The three of us ate in some wonderful restaurants and Mum probably drank more than she had ever in her life. She isn't a big drinker by any means, but Michael and I don't mind the odd tipple, and we've always been a bad influence!

On that Ireland trip Mum must have said 'What would my mother say of me if she saw me?' about a hundred times. Almost every day we'd start in an Irish pub in Dublin at 10am, drinking a pint of Guinness stout, and Mum would have a half pint and a cigarette. It was pretty funny, Mum got right into it.

I remember one night the three of us went to one Irish pub, which was due to shut at about 11pm. We weren't ready to go home for the night so Michael and I talked to the owner and they let us stay for a lock-in. We staggered out of there at 3am with Mum trailing behind us as sober as a judge, making sure her two crazy sons got home alright. She's dined out on that story ever since.

11

BREAD AND WINE

In all the restaurants I'd worked at—Two Faces, Roesti Bistro, The Waterside Inn and Kensington Place—I noticed that every owner would eat in their restaurant quite regularly. Hermann did it, Mr Roux and of course Rowley did too. I didn't know if it was out of necessity, convenience or to get a taste of what they were actually offering.

I now know it was mainly the latter. Perhaps because my role at KP allowed me to see the front line a bit more, I noticed that Rowley would eat in the dining room and get the full service. He wasn't spoiling himself; not in the slightest. He was monitoring his business.

Whether you're a chef or an owner it is very important to eat in your own restaurant as much as you can to appreciate and understand the customer's experience. I do it all the time now and I have done so in all of my businesses. I want to be treated like a guest and I want to try and see it through their eyes so I can better understand what it is we are actually giving to the guest.

The difference between what some operators are actually offering and what they think they are offering can be enormous. The perception of your product can be blurred by your own self-belief to succeed and sometimes you can't see what is actually going on. Sometimes a waiter will bring over a coffee that is spilt in the saucer without even blinking. And you have to ask, why am I getting that if I'm paying x amount of dollars?

It's very important that you sit, eat and watch how the restaurant is being served. Of course you'll never experience exactly what your guests experience because your staff are clued up enough to make sure everything is okay, or so you like to think. The key for me, just as it is for a restaurant critic I'm told, is to watch what is actually happening to the other diners in the room.

I send friends in undercover and reimburse them later as well. This is something I do once every two months at all my restaurants. I send them in, they have the full dining experience and then they write me an email describing everything that happens. It's important to understand what happens to guests, it's not always what you're expecting to hear. But it's what you need to hear to understand the business better.

So after seeing Rowley do it on a regular basis at KP, David and I decided it would be a good idea if we ate in the restaurant on one of our days off. We'd always wondered what the restaurant experience at KP was like, and why it was getting such rave reviews. We had a fair idea, but now it was time to get a taste for ourselves. So we booked for lunch and asked to sit on table 50. It's a lovely little table for two on a raised platform overlooking the restaurant. The prime position in the restaurant. All sounds a little too romantic doesn't it?

Although we were keen to experience the restaurant from the diner's view, the reality was we were going to eat well, drink lots of wine, relax and just enjoy the experience.

David and I really hit it off because we where always good at banter, we both had a cheeky streak and we always tried to outdo each other with the ladies then too. We were young lads out for a good time.

During lunch we noticed two American women dining in the room as well. They were a lot older than us, probably in their late thirties, and we were about 23. So I guess essentially they were a couple of cougars. Towards the end of lunch I invited them over for a couple of drinks, and then things got really interesting. The four of us were having a lot of fun so once we finished up we all went back to David's flat to continue the good times and have another drink. Not that we needed any more!

David had a bottle of 1962 Chateau Lafite Rothschild from a cooking gig on a pheasant shoot in Cornwell, given to him by Mr Rothschild from his private cellar. I think at the time it was worth over a thousand pounds, so as you'd imagine David was keeping it for a very special occasion.

David has made me aware on numerous occasions that he didn't plan on opening it that night, but sometimes when you've had a skinful, and you're trying to impress someone you do stupid things. So we opened it.

The four of us sat there on the floor. David decanted this amazing bottle of wine, and then I started talking and got all animated with my arms and accidentally knocked over the bloody bottle of wine. It

BREAD AND WINE

went all over the carpet! I looked at David and I'm pretty sure I had fear written all over my face, and he just looked at me stunned in disbelief. He looked like he could have killed me!

David has told the story about a million times since, so perhaps what happened next are best said in his words. 'Luke goes down on his hands and knees and he's there licking and sucking the bloody carpet! It was just a disaster, a thousand pound bottle of plonk and here's Luke sucking the carpet like a vacuum cleaner.'

Needless to say, the girls had no idea of the value of this wine, and once they saw me licking it up off the floor they thought, right these guys are insane, it's time to go home. We never saw them again. I'm not surprised.

We were certainly a couple of lunatics back then. We've been up to no good ever since, the only difference is our names have changed. He never calls me Luke and I never call him David; he calls me Gordon, and I call him Stevie. I know that might sound strange, but I christened him Stevie because he looks like Steve McGarrett off *Hawaii Five-O*. He begs to differ; perhaps it's my double vision.

As for me being named Gordon? Well it's got nothing to do with the 'F-word' Gordon, I can assure you. The nickname came about years after we met while we were both working in Sydney. At the time of the technology boom David and I were trading on all the in specie stocks on a daily basis for fun. We really had no idea what we were doing and were just punting and trying our luck, although we did get the odd tip from the guys who worked with the stock markets when they came in to eat. But we were probably losing more than we were making, so it shows how much they knew!

So to take the piss out of me, and perhaps to get back at me for calling him 'Stevie', David ended up calling me Gordon after the infamous Gordon Gecko, from Wall Street. Since then he's been Stevie and I've been Gordon. He's even in my phone as 'Stevie'. I've practically forgotten his name is David!

Back in the days at KP we spent a lot of time running amok, and it formed the basis of an irreplaceable friendship. Practically every night after work we would drink at The Palace.

One night a bunch of the sous chefs (who hated us mind you) joined David and I for pints and pool down at The Palace. It must have been about 4am, we were all plastered and I remember one of the chefs, Rod, was taking a shot at pool and he just passed out while bent over the pool table in the shooting position. Dave and I were in hysterics. We got home about 7am and rocked up to work an hour later for our shifts. We weren't laughing any more. What were we thinking?

As fate would have it we had the busiest lunch trade in years and the night service went into overdrive. We did 315 covers. I was on the grill and David was on the vegetables. We went through waves of nausea and were crook as dogs, but importantly, as stupid as that was, we still didn't fuck anything up or let anyone down. We slept well that night, I can tell you.

Although that was pretty dumb, one thing's for certain, you'd never drink during work, and never ever take drugs. Well certainly David or I didn't, but we certainly had our fair share of hangovers. I've never taken a drug, well perhaps one or two puffs on the peace pipe at the most, but of course I never inhaled... as one of my icons Bill Clinton once said.

Although David was English and it was his home country, we were both just backpackers with no money. We worked hard and we weren't paid a lot. What we were paid we basically pissed up against the wall or spent in a great restaurant. That's okay when you're young; you're just out for a good time. When you work as hard as we did at that age you have to go out and blow off some steam. Living in London, as anyone who has done it would agree, isn't cheap and a big percentage of our wages was on rent. We were living out of each other's pockets, literally. Sometimes we had to pay our rent with coins because it was that tight at the end of the week. Embarrassingly I even asked one of my best mates, Darren Barnett, for a 50 quid loan to help pay the rent. It was always a fine line.

Of course it probably didn't help that we drank more than our body weight every week. We just lived in the fast lane. David and I were always up to no good.

One night we had finished late at KP and headed off to The Palace for a few quiet beers. Of course we ended up having a skinful and made our way home at about 3am.

So here we were, a couple of young scallywags wondering through the streets in the middle of the night, when we came across a delivery van that was offloading baked goods to the hotel on the corner for the next day's trade. There was no one around and the roller door at the back of the van was open and it was jam-packed with baked goods.

When you have two young drunk idiots, both of whom have little or no money and a spontaneous and rebellious nature, then odds are there was only going to be one outcome in this scenario.

We had a quick look around, I jumped in the van and David said 'What the hell are you doing, Luke?'

I ran to the back of the van, grabbed two big brown sacks, threw one to David and we fucking legged it! Our hearts were racing, we couldn't stop laughing, it was madness. We were dropping bits and pieces as we ran down the street. The baker came out and saw us sprinting off with his stuff.

So he chased us. We turned the corner, jumped the fence and ducked straight into David's flat, turned the lights off and ducked down behind the counter. It was insane. We were trying not to piss ourselves laughing, trying to catch our breath and were hoping we were far enough ahead that the baker wouldn't have seen us go into the flat.

Then there was a *bang!* on the front door.

'You little pricks, I know you're in there,' he yelled.

We were packing it, but killing ourselves with laughter at the same time, and there was no way in hell we were going to open that door. We sat there as quiet as we could, and eventually the baker gave up.

Once the coast was clear David said 'come on, let's have a look and see what the hell we got.'

We turned on the kitchen light and opened up the bags. It was just Mother's Pride plain white sliced loaves of fucking bread! We were dreaming of nice baguettes, or pain au chocolates and croissants but there it was, cheap sliced bread. What an anticlimax! So much for seeing an opportunity and taking it. Serves us right. I've never eaten so much bread in my life. The stupid things you do when you are young!

12

ROWLEY GETS SNOOKERED, AND I GET BOWLED OVER

We were doing serious numbers at KP, around 300 a day. It was a well-oiled machine, and although I got on very well with Rowley, the gamut of higher-ranking chefs who hated me made me feel like I was never going to get anywhere. I was only at KP for about ten months when I realised enough was enough, there was no room for me to grow there.

Rowley could tell I wasn't enjoying it and I think he wanted to keep me because he liked what I could do. So he said he had a position down at his other restaurant Launceston Place (LP) that would suit my skills a little better. The position was junior sous chef. It was a major step up for me and gave me a sense of control in the kitchen.

I'd be running the meat and sauce section, as well as creating my own stocks and soups in a small team of seven chefs.

Before taking the new role I took a young American girl I'd met at the bar at KP one night down to LP to check it out and see what the place was like. At that stage I was only on 150 quid a week, and at LP you could easily spend that on two people for dinner. So I was very careful about what I ordered, and what we drank. When I asked for the bill the waiter informed me 'Chef Rowley has taken care of the bill, Sir.'

I felt like a star! A gift like that was bloody huge. It was a week's wages saved, and it certainly impressed the American girl as well.

More importantly, I really loved what they were trying to achieve at LP. The technique and approach taken with the food looked like an exciting challenge as well, so I took the gig.

Rowley agreed that David and I worked so well together it made sense we both made the move to Launceston Place. In the lead up to our big switch David and I took the opportunity to get away from the kitchen for a bit of a break.

It had been a pretty tough year at KP and we were feeling pretty burnt out. London goes pretty quiet just after Christmas and New Year, so Rowley let us take a five-day holiday.

David and I met at Heathrow airport on Boxing Day morning and took a flight down to Lisbon, Portugal. We went straight into party mode. It's a pretty quick flight but we had enough gin and tonic to not even notice that the plane had landed.

We disembarked the plane, grabbed our bags and David said, 'right, what the hell shall we do now?'

We had no plans. Nothing. It was all about getting on the plane and letting spontaneity take over. I've always thought the best adventures

ROWLEY GETS SNOOKERED, AND I GET BOWLED OVER

are unplanned. So here we were, in a country where neither of us had been before, drunk, and unable to speak Portuguese. I guess we were behaving like true backpackers; two young blokes looking for a good time.

We went and had a look at the information booth and decided to get a coach to the Algarve on the south coast. We had to wait five hours until the bus left. Drink anyone?

Algarve is about 250 kilometres from Lisbon. We got a couple of roadies and bunkered in for the long bus trip. About three hours in I was getting pretty fed up. David had passed out and I was wide awake, bored and uncomfortable. So I woke him up and said, 'right, I've had enough of this bus, I want to get off. Lets go.'

David squinted his eyes at me. 'What the hell?'

'I want to get off the bus.'

'We're in the bloody middle of nowhere, Luke, there aren't even any lights outside or anything,' he said.

It was too late. My mind was made up. 'I don't care. Come on, I'm sick of this bus ride, we're getting off.'

We put our backpacks on and walked down to the driver. I tapped him on the shoulder and said 'Can you stop? We want to get off, we've had enough.'

The coach driver pulled over. We jumped off in the middle of bloody god-knows-where; it was pitch black. The bus drove off.

'Luke, what the fuck are we doing?' David kept asking.

We ended up walking with our backpacks on, up and down all these hills, for god knows how many hours until we finally found a roadhouse of some description. We stayed there until first light.

After talking to some of the locals we jumped in a cab down to a place called Albufeiram, which is kind of the gateway to the Algarve.

We stayed at a little tennis club for all four nights of the trip. We were madmen; all we did was party hard all night before rising in the morning, or more often mid-morning, then chilling out and curing our hangovers by feasting on the local delicacies before firing up and partying again.

The second morning we both had an almighty hangover. We had met a couple of locals the night before and they had us drinking some provincial liquid that no doubt doubles as tractor fuel. I thought tequila was evil, but this stuff… it made me wonder how we were still alive.

To help shake off the hangover jitters we grabbed a bite to eat down on the harbour. At this tiny little café we had coffees and the most amazing pain au chocolate ever. Nothing has beaten it since. We weren't even in France! It certainly made us feel better.

It was a glorious morning, the sun was out and the water a crystal blue so we went for a walk on the beach. We were strolling along and came across this fisherman with a full sack of sardines that he'd just caught. He showed us the bag and explained he was about to cook some up on the beach. He had this little barbecue he'd built in the sand. Some of the locals joined in and offered us drinks while he filleted the sardines on the sand in front of us. He used just a bit of olive oil and grilled them up, and we spent the morning sitting on the sand eating the most succulent and fresh sardines I've ever experienced. I'm not sure I've had a better breakfast ever. It proved that clean, fresh and simple food is impossible to beat.

We returned to London and joined the team at LP for a fresh start. KP was a massive restaurant by any measure, but LP was a small corner restaurant with only about 60 seats plus a private dining room. It was more refined; it was fine dining in every sense.

ROWLEY GETS SNOOKERED, AND I GET BOWLED OVER

LP was a restaurant that the 'who's who' of the UK dined at, and they dined regularly. Lady Diana, Michael Parkinson, Prince Andrew, Sarah Ferguson, Elton John... it was insane. Every night a message would come into the kitchen saying something like 'Elton John is on 44, make sure everything is alright.' It was pretty wild.

The kitchen at LP was in the basement, and it was so tiny it was as if I'd gone back in time to the kitchen at Two Faces. Seven chefs would spin, turn and pivot while producing every dish.

Although we no longer worked together, my mate Gus came down from The Waterside Inn on Mondays to continue our ritual of eating in a Michelin-starred restaurant on our day off. At this stage I was renting out a 50-quid-a-week room in someone's house off Ladbroke Grove in Kensington. It was a pretty small room. Half the time Gus would stay the night, and more often than not I'd wake up on Tuesday morning and he'd be sitting asleep on the chair, fully clothed. I'd wake him up, then he'd rush off to get the train back to Bray for his Tuesday double shift.

About a month into the gig at LP, Gus couldn't make the Monday lunch so Rowley and I decided we would go and check out Antony Worrall Thompson's restaurant down in Notting Hill Gate.

Rowley and I got on very well. It was the sort of relationship that I'd never had with a boss before; we were more friends than anything. When we had lunch it didn't take much arm-twisting to get stuck into some pretty nice wines.

We got pretty damn pissed, and as we left the restaurant Rowley suggested we go down the road and have a game of snooker. The more we drank, the more we talked about food. Feeling pretty confident about the job I was doing at LP, I said 'Rowley, I want to talk about my wages. I don't think I'm being paid enough.'

'Oh yeah? What do you expect you should be on?' he asked.

I said 'I want 250 pounds a week, I want to do eight shifts a week and I want to do those shifts from Monday to Thursday as four doubles—all straight up.'

In those days we had a problem, or perhaps *I* had a problem, with chefs swapping sections. You'd come in to do your shift and the section was a mess from the other chef. Preparation is vital to the success of any service, no matter what level. I thought if I had complete control of my section for every shift then everything would be exactly how I wanted it, and it would run as smoothly as possible. I was pretty anal about my whole mise en place; Hermann and Mr Roux had drilled that into me, and it stuck.

'No, it's too much,' Rowley replied. 'I'll give you 180 pounds and you can have it for seven shifts.'

I wasn't budging. 'No, I want to do eight shifts and I want 250 quid. I'll play you a game of snooker for it?'

He laughed. 'Alright, we'll play for it.'

We were blind drunk mind you, and it was probably the world's longest snooker game. Somehow I won. Whether he let me win I don't know, but I was pretty pleased with myself.

After our epic snooker battle we stumbled our way back to Rowley's place for a bit of a night cap or three. It must have been about one or two in the morning, and we were sitting there enjoying a nice vino when he asked 'Do you like golf Luke?'

'Um, yeah.'

'Good,' he replied as he got up and made his way to the spare room. He came out with a bag of golf clubs.

We then went out on the street, outside his house. I put the ball down in the middle of the road and had a swing. Sparks flew off the asphalt. I hit something on a house down the road and it made an

ROWLEY GETS SNOOKERED, AND I GET BOWLED OVER

almighty *bang!* All the lights came on so we legged it! A guy in his twenties and his boss in his late 30s acting like a pack of troublesome teens. It was pretty funny, we certainly had a great day.

Rowley lived up to his word and I got my eight shifts, consecutive doubles, and I got a salary that meant I could start to try and save a bit too.

Only a few days later I met someone who changed the course of my life forever. While I was working in the meat butchery section, the LP restaurant manager and owner, Nick Smallwood, walked through the kitchen with this young attractive woman who was introduced as a new front of house staff member.

In those days I was young and trying to get the attention of attractive girls, any girl really. Nick knew what I was like so when he came over to me he said 'This is Lucy Allon, she is going to be one of our new assistant restaurant managers.' He then turned to Lucy and said 'Stay away from this boy, he's always up to no good.'

I couldn't have paid him for a better endorsement, really. Lucy had graduated from university but hospitality had always intrigued her. LP was her first job in a real fine dining restaurant, and Nick really took her under his wing.

The kitchen at LP was in the basement, so we'd ring a bell and send the food up in a dumb waiter. David Rayner was on the pass so he was the one in control of sending the food up, and it was Lucy's job to collect it and take it out to guests.

I was pretty interested in Lucy so I started sending up little notes with the meals to try and get her attention. I'd ask her to go out on a date with me, or say something like, *I finish at 11pm, what time do you knock off? Let's go and grab a drink.*

On one note I wrote *Can I take you to lunch at La Tante Claire?* La Tante Claire was Pierre Koffman's three Michelin star restaurant at the time, and is now Gordon Ramsay's. David sent the note up with the next meal. Soon enough the dumb waiter came back down with a message from Lucy that David read out loud. *I've already been there*, it said. The whole kitchen laughed. She's always had a very sharp mind.

I was very persistent and eventually she gave in. We went on a date to a place called Beach Blanket Babylon in Notting Hill and hit it off immediately. Lucy and I started dating, but neither of us had any idea that just a year or so down the track we would create a formidable business partnership.

Lucy accepted a job as assistant manager at a new restaurant named Ransome's Dock run by a successful restaurateur Martin Lamb, and I continued to work at LP over the summer. However, I knew my time in the UK was drawing to an end.

PART TWO

'Success is the ability to go from failure to failure without losing your enthusiasm.'

Sir Winston Churchill

13

ROGUES TO RICHES

In 1993 my visa had run its course and it was time to head home. England had given me a fresh perspective on life, a wealth of culinary skills and, more importantly, instilled a lot of confidence in my cheffing ability. I'd spent years in some of England's best restaurants, learning from culinary kings Roux and Leigh, and it was time to see what opportunities the culinary world held for me back home.

Lucy had never been to Australia, and she was keen to see what it offered for her career and lifestyle. I came back to Australia first with the intention of creating a base, while Lucy continued on in London for a few months to organise her working visa.

My brother Michael was working at Pier Nine in Brisbane at the time. He got me a job with an old friend of his in a huge restaurant on the river that pumped out massive numbers every service. The money was really good, but it was tourist trade and there was no scope to be creative. It was 300 covers a service at an average standard, and I just looked at it as an opportunity to find my feet and get a bit of coin in the bank. Every cent I had earned in the UK was spent eating in restaurants or on the amber fluid at the local pub, so it was well and truly time to try and save. That job in Brisbane was short-lived; really, deep down, I hated it. I wanted to move somewhere where I had more of a creative scope and a strong belief in what we were trying to achieve.

Before Lucy moved to Australia she came out for a holiday to get a taste for life down under. To say Lucy hated Brisbane is an understatement. We agreed if she was to move out here, then we would move to Melbourne and see what the food capital of Australia had to offer. Given both of our strong appetites to succeed in the industry, the plan made perfect sense.

Lucy moved to Australia on 1 December, 1993. We set up residence in Melbourne without any jobs. David Rayner moved out as well and the three of us shared a brand new two bedroom flat in the suburb of Balaclava.

Within no time at all Lucy scored a waiting job with chef Ian Curley who was manning the pans at Rhubarbs in Gertrude Street. David landed a solid job as well. As for me, well, I had a couple of different opportunities, but one after the other they would just fall over. Everything I touched turned into nothing but a dead end.

The first was Cafe Kanis in Richmond. I was given the opportunity to be sous chef under a chef whose name escapes me, but although he'd left before I arrived, Andrew Blake had made it famous. Sadly it closed down two months after I arrived. The second was a new venture, Hats Restaurant with Harry Hajisava as chef and Tony

Cetinic in the front of house. Hats opened in the wrong location on Toorak Road and had nothing more than tumbleweed roll through its doors. It closed just as quickly as it opened.

I even went for a job at Stephanie Alexander's restaurant, Stephanie's at Hawthorn, in the old mansion. The position was sous chef, but I didn't get the gig. I was very nervous going for the interview because she is a legend of Australian food. She gave me a tour of the kitchen and showed me around. Stephanie is very direct and firm, and I don't think we would have got on. I'm very cheeky, well, a brat at times I guess, and I'm not sure she would have put up with me.

Stephanie has been an inspiration to countless generations of food lovers, and the introduction of The School Kitchen Garden Project, which focuses on the food education of children, is a testament to the drive, passion and dedication of the woman. She is one of the great culinary heroes who gave Australia a chance, along with people like Hermann Schneider, Gloria Staley, Gay Bilson, Tony Bilson, Mietta O'Donnell, Phillip Searle and Cheong Liew. They set up a platform, a springboard for the next generation, who at that time were about to explode onto the scene and draw the focus of the world down under; young guns like Neil Perry who was already making his mark, then Kylie Kwong, Tetsuya Wakuda and Peter Doyle.

As for me, however, in 1993 I couldn't even land a job. Was it all just bad luck, bad timing or was I making the wrong decisions? I was becoming pretty disillusioned. The UK had been so positive, and everything seemed to just fall into place. I had such a great social life and work dynamic there, but in Australia I was beginning to question whether I would be bouncing from job to job for the rest of my life.

The problem was there wasn't anything else I could do. I felt like a complete dunce. I basically had to be a chef, it's all I knew.

Life in Melbourne just out and out sucked. I couldn't hold down a job, and I was beginning to question if Australia was really for me. Lucy and I decided that if it wasn't going to work out we'd seriously consider going back to England. I was so close to actually throwing in cooking!

A phone call was to change all that.

I'd applied for a position, advertised in the paper, for a sous chef at a new venture named Rogues that involved one of Australia's finest chefs, Neil Perry. At the same time Mr Roux was in Australia and had been to Rockpool in Sydney for dinner. Owner Neil Perry told Mr Roux that he was at a bit of a loose end trying to find a chef for Rogues on the bustling Oxford street site. Mr Roux told Neil that I, one of his protégés, was back in Australia and could be the answer to all his problems. The timing couldn't have been better. I got a phone call from Neil asking me to come in for an interview. It was the best news I'd had since arriving back home.

Lucy and I sat down and discussed whether Sydney was an option. Australia was going through a really exciting time with food at that stage, and we felt we wanted to be a part of what was happening if we could. And from what we'd heard, Sydney had a lot more to offer opportunity-wise.

Lucy had a great job at Rhubarbs, and I didn't want to ruin her career ambitions, but Lucy was always pretty open-minded and suggested there was no harm in at least coming up to Sydney for a weekend. Plus, she didn't want to come all the way to Australia and go back to England without having visited Sydney at least once.

I borrowed $500 from my mum so we could get the bus to Sydney for the interview. Neil invited us in for dinner so we could get a first-hand experience of the restaurant in full operation.

The atmosphere at Rogues was busy and buzzy and the food was right on the money. Neil came out to the table towards the end of the evening, joined us for a glass of wine and offered me the position of sous chef.

I explained that we were Melbourne-based, that Lucy had a great job down there and it wasn't that simple to accept. I was keen as hell, but moving from Melbourne was a big commitment. I wasn't going to take the job in Sydney unless Lucy could get a job in Sydney as well. Neil thought that was fair enough, so he immediately offered her a waiting position at Rockpool.

It all sounded perfect. So I shook his hand and took the job.

We moved up to Sydney straight away, and because we had nowhere to live yet we slept on a floor of a friend's apartment for the first few weeks. It was so intense working, living on the floor and trying to find somewhere to live in a new city, but after a month we finally found an apartment in Potts Point to move into. Lucy was loving the challenge of Rockpool and Rogues was busy as hell.

This was the first time I met Kylie Kwong. She was working for Neil at the time at Rogues in the lead up to the launch of Wokpool, for which Neil and Kylie would become renowned.

One Thursday night, we were all busy working towards the end of yet another successful night's trade when a tall gentleman in a suit came in the kitchen and demanded to know who cooked his dinner. I didn't know what to think. I got my back up and said, 'I did, was there a problem?'

He said that was one of the best meals he'd eaten in Sydney in the last ten years, perhaps a little too French and a bit too heavy, but he really enjoyed it. He gave me his business card and said 'let's keep in contact. If ever you need anything in Sydney, let me know.'

I put the card in my back pocket, got on with cooking and thought nothing of it. I'd seen it all before, and I've seen it since. People come into your restaurant all self-important, offer you a million things, promise to do business and then you never hear from them again. I'd seen it happen to Hermann at Two Faces, I'd see it happen to Mr Roux at Waterside Inn, and to Rowley Leigh at Kensington Place. It's just one of those things. You be polite and hope they come back to dine at your restaurant, but rarely does it eventuate in business.

The following morning was a Friday, the best day in the restaurant industry for trade. Lunch service is always big and the night service is even bigger. When you work in the industry it's the day you crave: the energy, the non-stop frenetic activity and the wonderful sense of achievement that filters through your bones at the end of a long double shift.

When I arrived at Rogues at 8am I was locked out.

Just when I thought I'd got on a roll, without any warning whatsoever the business had gone bust. Locks had been placed overnight, and there was nothing we could do about it. Fucking hell, bad luck was chasing me around like a bad smell.

I was devastated. I rang Lucy, who was down at Rockpool setting up for lunch. Staff are not normally allowed phone calls unless it's an emergency so she was short with me on the phone. She said 'what do you want? Make it really quick.'

'There's fucking padlocks on the door! What am I supposed to do?'

As usual Lucy provided a calming influence, but I honestly thought I was on the verge of throwing it all in. There was nothing we could do. We couldn't even give all of our customers who had booked a courtesy call to let them know we were not open for business. It was a catastrophe. Another restaurant, and another failure for my career. Was it just me?

Neil was a consultant to the project only, something I wasn't really aware of at the time, and for various reasons he'd pulled out of the restaurant, and just a few weeks after there were padlocks on the doors.

Of course, one thing I've learned about life is that when one door closes, if you have your eyes wide open, sure enough another door will open almost instantaneously.

For some unknown reason I remembered the gentleman from the night before who kindly thanked me for the meal. I went back home and had a rummage around for the card. It was in the back pocket of my chef pants sitting in the laundry basket; thankfully I'd left for work in the morning without putting a load of washing on. I pulled the card out. The name of the gentleman was John Hemmes—one of Australia's most influential hospitality businessmen.

14

THE BIG BREAK

Although I had no idea Rogues was doomed, apparently John 'Mr John' Hemmes knew. It was the reason he came in for dinner that night before it closed.

With nothing to lose I got on the blower to Mr John. 'I've heard about you. You worked in London with the Roux brothers, and that is why Neil Perry brought you up to Rogues. Those are very good credentials,' he said.

Mr John and his wife Merivale were embarking on an epic project to refurbish the old four-storey National Bank building in the central business district of Sydney on the corner of King and York, boldly called CBD. There was to be a bar on the ground floor, restaurant on the second, the third would have a private club and the fourth was solely for private functions.

They'd secured the site for around $3 million and Mr John was searching for a chef who matched his vision. So what the hell was he talking to me for, I wondered. Sure, I'd trained under Hermann, Mr Roux and Rowley Leigh, but I hadn't had a solid job for nigh on a year. I was only 24 and still had a lot to learn.

Neil Perry had made Rogues a very French restaurant, something I was pretty happy about because all my training had a strong French backbone. As I'd come to learn, Mr John certainly doesn't pull any punches. He said to me 'Your food is a little too French for my liking, it's too heavy for what I'm looking for.' He wanted food with a strong technical background, like French, but merged towards modern Australian with a certain spark to get people's attention. He wanted the hottest restaurant in town, and someone to push the boundaries in the kitchen.

Mr John originally had another chef in mind for CBD: Gerard Madani from the Intercontinental. He had a very big name here but he'd scored a green card to work in the USA. Mr John looked everywhere, including in Melbourne, Perth and Brisbane, but couldn't find anyone who he thought fit his vision. He had his hopes on me, but he wasn't convinced yet.

To get a better understanding of my food Mr John offered me a job at Merivale, one of his restaurants in Potts Point. I was rapt. One thing I've learned is that if opportunity is in front of you grab it by the horns and hang on. I may never be the best chef in the world, but if I don't do it, someone else will. You never know if you don't try.

After about a month, however, I was getting pissed off as I didn't know where my future was going. The new gig at CBD sounded exciting so I put pressure on Mr John.

He still didn't know whether I was what he wanted for the epic CBD project. 'I'm not sure Luke, I haven't really seen your food yet.'

THE BIG BREAK

I said 'Well, I don't want to show all my recipes here. How about I do some specials tomorrow for you to try?'

I made three specials. It was some time ago now and my memory is a tad blurry, but I know one of the dishes I cooked was a ravioli of prawn with tomato, basil, lemon and olive oil. Mr John was blown away. He described my food that day as 'advanced', 'very original' and 'simple but beautifully balanced'.

So he finally gave me the job. I got an amazing salary, a car and a place to live all in the package. I was back, baby!

To celebrate, Mr John invited me to dine across the road from Merivale at Peter Doyle's Trianon. In the following year Peter and his wife renovated the property, changed the name to Cicada and took the restaurant world by storm. And to this day Peter Doyle is one of the most respected chefs in the country. He's very passionate and one of my favourite chefs.

I asked Mr John if I could bring my girlfriend Lucy. During dinner Lucy told Mr John how she met me in London and had worked at Ransome's Dock under Martin Lamb when it won an award for the best service in Britain. Mr John was impressed, and it wasn't long before Lucy left Rockpool. The two of us would soon make a formidable team, just as we'd hoped for upon leaving England. Not only were we going to run a restaurant together, we had the chance to create a restaurant from the ground up.

I remember drinking my first glass of Krug Champagne while we celebrated. Amazing. Just a month after I was considering chucking it all in, here I was drinking the best French champagne, having scored an amazing job.

We had a period of about eight months between leaving Rogues and CBD actually opening its doors. Lucy and I would go into The

Forbes Hotel, a tiny little pub diagonally opposite CBD, and sit on this tiny two-seater table on the balcony on the first floor facing the building. We'd sit there for hours, looking across and talking about what we wanted to do with the service, how we would do this and that. Really, we sat there sipping wine, planning our restaurant destiny.

We chose all the furnishings, and bought the chairs and the menus. CBD was the first of the real pub restaurants and embodied that casual, yet serious, dining atmosphere: polished floorboards, white linen tablecloths, a big open bar and staff who were affable, but knew what they were doing.

There were the usual delays because it was a new build, but the new challenge for me was being able to design the kitchen at CBD. It was a tight space. All of the kitchens I have worked in had been very streamlined, and having that ability to be involved in the design and build meant I could place all of my equipment in a manner to get the best productivity.

We opened on Valentine's Day, 14 February 1994.

In many ways CBD was an incarnation of Kensington Place. I had realised that simple combinations and attention to how you cook are really the best. So all the food I've ever created is food I love to eat: simple clean flavours. Having said that, at CBD I had to be very creative. It was my first head chef role in Australia's largest city, working for Mr John, who was arguably the most successful hospitality businessman in Australia. So there was this air of expectation on the food as well.

Rowley Leigh was often the pass at Kensington Place. Nothing left the kitchen at The Waterside Inn without the chef on the pass too. It is how great kitchens must run. It was my role to not only cook in the kitchen, but to manage the pass and ensure every dish that

THE BIG BREAK

left the galley was up to scratch. I loved the responsibility. Sure there were times when I was rude, aggressive: a tyrant. I was pretty tough, but you need to be when you are trying to create something different from every other chef. Your reputation is on the line.

I couldn't have been that tough though. One day, a young bright-eyed 16-year-old walked into CBD with a skateboard under his arm. His name was Shannon Binnie. I took one look at him and thought: *fuck, he's way too young*. I asked him if this is really what he wanted to do. Without batting an eyelid he said 'Yes.' So I gave the young kid a chance. He was the best I'd ever employed. Shannon would be the first in the kitchen in the morning and the last to leave, all by choice. 16 years later that tiny kid is now a partner in my restaurant Salt Tokyo. Who would have believed it?

Truth be known though, not every chef is 100 per cent committed to the cause. Every chef tries to sneak something through the gatekeeper because they are busy, under the pump or just plain lazy. It could be something as simple as they haven't cooked the beans properly, they've under-seasoned something, something is a bit overcooked, but they haven't the time to do another one. It's your job on the pass to make sure nothing slips through. It's your livelihood if you drop your standards and let that through. You have to be the eyes and ears of the kitchen.

I did have a fierce temper in the kitchen though, and Lucy had to moderate my effect on the front of house team. I would get a bit hot headed and if something went wrong during service I'd want it dealt with there and then, whereas Lucy's philosophy was a bit more rational. She would say 'Let's do what we have to do to get through this and make sure the customer is okay. Let's get through service and then deal with it.'

CBD was my first head chef role. I was 24 and still had a hell of a lot to learn, but at the same time I've always believed if someone gives you an opportunity the ball is in your court to prove they made the right decision. I was pretty confident at that stage. Although I'd had rotten luck in Melbourne, England had changed me. The years under culinary heavyweights had given me a strong resolve and belief in my capabilities.

Here I was, a skinny little opinionated chef employing guys that were 30 or 35, all to work under me and obey my command. That's pretty dangerous in a room full of egos. We had a lot of chefs that showed no respect towards me because they felt they had a lot more experience than I did. That may well have been the case but the fact was I was hired as head chef, like it or lump it. Some chefs were better cooks than me, but I was there to manage the team as much as anything, so I had to be strong and do it my way. I soon learned a lot about managing staff.

I made some poor decisions, but it hardened me up and also made me learn to back myself. Even if you make a wrong call, at the end of the day as the head chef you need to stick to your guns, because the buck stops with you.

In some ways I became an incarnation of Hermann. I was young and the only way to get the respect of the kitchen was to treat it like the fucking miltary. I had to build my own army of kitchen soldiers, prepared to obey my orders and deliver on our promise to the diner.

My attitude was, and still is, if you want the job and the opportunity you don't ask me how many hours you want to work, you don't ask me what your pay rise will be. You get in my kitchen, peel some fucking mushrooms, work hard, show me what you can do and then we'll talk about it.

THE BIG BREAK

One thing I've learned about restaurants is that it's a tough bloody business. The margins are low and the hours are long, and for a business to turn a profit it relies on everyone in the team. There's no point having one or two chefs who aren't on the same page as the others. If you have just one disruptive person it can throw off the performance of the whole team. My management goal has always been to get rid of that disruptive person as soon as you find him or her because it's like a cancer that spreads.

Lucy was on the floor and I was in the kitchen. It was great preparation for running our own restaurant. There is no doubt that Mr John had offered me my biggest break. I cannot thank him enough. I have nothing but respect for the man. He had a massive impact on the way I do business and manage my staff: firm but fair.

Before CBD I was merely 'a chef', but at CBD I became 'the chef'. The media attention became a complete circus.

15

CLASS OF 95

It wasn't long before we became a hotspot for the city's sinners, stockbrokers and soapie stars. Tom Cruise even celebrated one of his birthdays in the restaurant. He and Nicole Kidman had been in to eat at CBD on a few occasions, and every single time Tom ordered the grilled barramundi.

They were great days for me to get grounded and get settled in Sydney, and it gave me the confidence and resolve to take on the world. Our first review gave us a 15 out of 20 and came with the status of a coveted *SMH Good Food Guide* chef's hat, a recognition bestowed upon the best eateries in the city. Lucy and I were so proud of what we had created, and no doubt Mr John was too.

In 1995 Terry Durack wrote a piece in the *Sydney Morning Herald* called 'Class of '95'. He tabled the best new restaurants and explained

CLASS OF 95

why 1995 was 'the year for Sydney dining'. There was a bevy of amazing chefs who made the grade and the *Herald* did a photo shoot with about 30 of us, like a school photo, including culinary luminaries such as Janni Kyritsis, Neil Perry, Kylie Kwong—and me. The photo that appeared in the paper saw me poking my tongue out like a cheeky brat! What a muppet!

The same year, Lucy and I appeared in a piece entitled 'People to Watch'. I was getting a lot of media attention and barely a week went by that I wouldn't be interviewed for some sort of magazine, paper, radio or television program. As I started to get a bit of press I felt the pressure. Because of my youth, people were looking to see if I would fall in a heap, if I was a flash in the pan, or whether I was the real deal and able to sustain it.

For me though, CBD was just damn hard work. My priority was always to ensure the business was successful: the media profile was a bonus. Because of the city lunch trade, CBD had that really fast-paced service that KP had. The adrenalin pumps through your veins as you bash out the dishes and there was never a lull. It would shoot out of the gates at midday and we wouldn't catch our breath until 3pm… every day.

I designed the food to be really high-end brasserie style, not unlike KP, which is quick for waiters to get out but really polished with simple, bold flavours. The menu was fairly long by lunch standards, so it gave enough variety that we'd see people coming in twice a week. We had a great core of regulars.

Dinners were a nightmare though. Dinner trade in the city, especially back then, was really just pushing shit uphill. Weekday nights would be quiet and then you'd get a big crowd on Friday night, mainly plastered stockbrokers who had a lot of money to spend but no manners.

LUKE MANGAN

Mr Roux came over to Australia while I was head chef at CBD. Keen to see what one of his protégés was up to, he booked a table for two and dined with his wife Robyn. I'm not sure I've ever been as nervous as I was that night. It was the first time he'd experienced what I had achieved since I left The Waterside Inn.

He tried a dish that I was getting known for, and would eventually be considered a signature dish. I love mushrooms, and I love ginger, so I created a ginger sauce for this tart. We'd take a rabbit fillet and marinate it in a little bit of sesame seed and olive oil, then we grilled it, sliced it and put it on gooey, soft polenta with Parmesan in a tart shell. We placed a bit of sautéed shiitake mushrooms on top and finished with a rabbit-based jus with ginger through it. People went crazy for it.

Thankfully Mr Roux loved it. In fact, he loved it so much he made some favourable comments in the press, which caught the attention of Sydney. One of the best chefs in the world comes over here and talks about how impressed he was with your dish: boy, money can't buy that sort of advertising for your restaurant. The rabbit tart became an unexpected hit, and a drawcard for new clientele.

In 2010, some 16 years after that dinner at CBD, Mr Roux invited me to his house for dinner in the south of France. I was on a food voyage with my partner Belinda and a group of my closest mates to celebrate my 40th birthday. Although we'd always kept in touch I'd never been to Mr Roux's house for dinner, so I was a bit excited.

Belinda and I decided to hire a mini moke and enjoy the open air on the way down to his place. When we arrived we toured the house and then the four of us—Mr Roux, his wife Robyn, Belinda and I—played a bit of boules. He is just as competitive now as he was back when I worked at The Waterside Inn.

We had a ball, and then it was time for the highlight of the evening: back to the house for dinner. He showed me his cellar, which was huge: burgundies, chateau petrus, champagne, it was incredible. I've never seen anything like it.

He said 'So Luke, what would you like to drink tonight?'

'Well, it's your cellar Mr Roux, you pick.' I said.

'Please, call me Michel,' he said. 'What about we have some Champagne?'

He pulled out a bottle of Magnum Krug 1982. Get out of town.

We took it upstairs and drank it, but it wasn't long before we went back downstairs and he said 'What do you prefer, Burgundy or Bordeaux?'

I said 'I like Burgundy.'

We proceeded to have a La Tache DRC 1992, Richebourg DRC 1986, Louis Jadot Beaune Chouacheux 2002, Chateau d'Yquem 1988, a nightcap of Caribbean rum, in cask 1945 and Rum Trois Rivieres 1953.

Robyn cooked a beautiful sea bass with lentils, and then Mr Roux cooked a main course of roast chicken, roast potatoes, green beans and the most amazing French cheeses. We smoked cigars: 15-year-old Monte Cristo Nu 1. It was one of those experiences that I'll never forget.

That night he told me 'You've done me proud. I'm very proud of what you have done and what you've achieved.'

Mr Roux didn't have to do that—to have us at his home and spoil us with his and Robyn's wonderful hospitality. I'm forever indebted to Mr Roux. I wouldn't be where I am without him, Hermann, Rowley and Mr John: all incredible men.

While I might have pulled the rabbit dish out of my hat to much success, I pulled my most recognised dish out of somewhere else.

LUKE MANGAN

Rightly or wrongly, my most famous dish is probably the liquorice parfait. We still serve this in my restaurants now. It was spawned in the kitchen of CBD after months of trial and error.

While the majority of the menu at CBD was about solid performers with a bit of a twist, I was always trying to do something different with a dish or two and add a bit of a surprise factor. And I guess the liquorice parfait was the result of this dire need to be adventurous.

I first tried it with cinnamon, but that didn't work, and because I love liquorice so much we gave that a go. We tried it with chopped liquorice, but that was a failure. We ended up melting it through cream very slowly, and that was that.

After you make your sabayon, you melt the cream and liquorice, let it cool, blend it, pass it then fold it through as you would when making a nice light parfait. We did that with the liquorice cream and then we moulded it up. We tried serving it with mandarins, oranges and banana—all sorts of things. But we added a sugar syrup with lime in it and candied zest, a few lime segments, and it was like gold. It's as close to a savoury dessert as you'll get and for me it's perfect. It's rich and creamy, but you also have the lime cutting through that. Even those who don't like liquorice often find out they actually like this dessert.

My head chef at glass brasserie, Joe Pavlovich, keeps saying it is a bit old-fashioned and he's probably right, but when the balance of flavours work why change it! He still takes the piss out of me to this day.

The whole process of creating a dish is exciting. It's what you live for as a chef: balancing flavours, combinations and techniques to let the produce stand up proud and show you what it's capable of. I learned from Hermann, Mr Roux and Rowley how important it is to use and understand seasonal produce. I'd only use food I liked as well:

just because it was in season didn't mean it got a run on the menu.

We tried some crazy dishes at CBD. I loved this cured duck breast dish we served with a Campari jelly and a five-spice dressing. It was weird, but it kind of worked. Well I thought it did anyway.

CBD was frantic and I needed some time out. Darren Barnett and I were always mad golfers, so we decided to fly to Thailand for a holiday and play a bit of golf while we were there.

We flew into Bangkok and then on to Phuket, but on the way we hit major turbulence. The air hostesses were running around telling everyone to sit down and things were flying through the air. It was pretty concerning. I clenched my arm rests and Darren turned to me with a big smile and said 'This is it mate, we're going down.'

Thankfully it was short-lived and we arrived safe and sound. We had a ball in Phuket. We dined at the Baan Rim Pa restaurant on Phuket Island, which sadly ended up being washed away by the tsunami on Boxing Day in 2004. It was there that I first experienced an incredible dessert of freshwater chestnuts in a bowl of chilled coconut milk. It was amazing and inspired me to do my own interpretation of it at CBD and, later, Salt.

Somehow we signed up for and played in a small-time Phuket golf tournament. We both got these caddies carrying our bags around for the whole day as if we were pros. We were hacks though. This amazing storm broke and chased us up the 18th hole, there was a downpour and we had to putt out in six inches of water. It was crazy.

As expected, my stomach didn't hold up with all the spicy food and I became very ill. I was in my room for two whole days. Darren was getting worried and said 'Mate, we have to fix you up, this isn't good.' He took me to some strange bloody poor excuse for a chemist on Phuket Island. Of course the chemists in Phuket aren't quite like the ones you get on the corner in Australia.

We told the chap behind the counter what was wrong and he handed over all these vials filled with powder. It was a bit frightening. He said 'Here take this powder, and this powder.' I had no idea what I was consuming.

Darren thought it was hilarious and I remember him saying 'Whatever you do, make sure you don't take it back on the plane with us. We may end up in the Bangkok Hilton.'

Back in Sydney, Lucy and I had well and truly found our feet. CBD was doing really well and we scraped together enough cash to buy a terrace house in Paddington for $285,000. Life was pretty good.

However, although the restaurant was churning like a well-oiled machine, we were working really long hours and it was all getting a bit monotonous. Mr John was a good boss but once he sees success he wants to channel it, he doesn't want to tinker with it. If it ain't broke, don't fix it. That makes complete sense, but Lucy and I started to get a bit restless. We had matured quite a bit through the four years at CBD and it was time for a new challenge.

If we are working this hard, we thought, why don't we do it for ourselves?

In 1997 we first asked the Merivale group whether we could buy into CBD, but they knocked us back. We were very open and told them we were interested in opening our own restaurant, and asked if they would be interested in backing that. They said no. By then they knew we were getting itchy feet and so Mr John was open to discussions on ideas for keeping us there.

One of the ideas was building a wall around the staircase to block out the noise coming up from the bar beneath. We also wanted a proper separate dining room entrance so our guests didn't have to walk through the pub if they didn't want to. Then we could make it a destination at night without having the effect of the bar: essentially its own premise.

They didn't like that idea either. We thought, well, we can't do this any more. The evenings were no longer enjoyable. They were either tediously quiet or very busy because the bar was full and everyone was pissed. We yearned for a change.

At that stage, Stan Sarris approached us because he was in the process of piecing together one of Australia's most significant restaurants, Banc. We had quite an intense conversation. It seemed like a very exciting opportunity, but I think deep down Lucy and I were concerned about how we would work with Stan. He really wanted to be in control and we knew that we wanted to do our own thing. Stan's idea and concept for Banc was very strong and very clear, but we felt that we would be fulfilling Stan Sarris's dream, rather than our own.

I remember Stan Sarris bringing Rodney Adler into CBD for lunch to taste my food. It was pretty close, and we even walked through the empty shell of the restaurant to get a feel for the place. We went and looked at it and both Lucy and I were pretty fucking near to going ahead. But it all came down to gut feeling. It just didn't feel right. It didn't feel like our dream.

That was one of the best things that we didn't do. Because what Liam Tomlin did with Banc was amazing, and there's been a lot of amazing chefs come out of that as well: Justin North, Matthew Kemp, Warren Turnbull and Colin Fassnidge. It was an incredible institution.

At least Lucy and I were a bit clearer in our minds with what we wanted to do. We knew if we left CBD we would do something on our own, just the two of us in control. We wanted to be masters of our own destiny and create our own thing from the ground up. We didn't know what it would be yet but the ball was already rolling, so we decided it was time to leave CBD, take some time off, and work out what the hell we were going to do.

I asked Mr John if we could have lunch. I planned to tell him after we were well lubricated. He agreed and suggested we go to Damien Pignolet's Bistro Moncur.

Mr John knew we were a bit restless and had already heard rumours that we were looking around. When we met at Bistro Moncur Mr John spoke before I could get a word in. 'I already know you are leaving me.'

'That's right,' I replied.

He said 'Don't worry about it Luke, I'm organised already for you to leave.'

'If you're organised who is going to take it over?' I asked.

Mr John asked if the chef could join us from the kitchen. He introduced him as Matthew Flemming, my replacement. The wily old fox! We both laughed, Mr John ordered a bottle of Champagne and we had a great lunch. A long, long lunch. There were no hard feelings. The CBD days were over and I'd graduated in the Sydney dining scene, but I had no idea what my next step would be.

Liquorice Parfait with Lime Syrup

Serves 6

Lime Syrup
100ml sugar
2 limes, juiced
2 limes, zested

Liquorice Parfait
240ml cream
50g liquorice
2 eggs
2 yolks
15g glucose
60g sugar
10ml Pernod

Tuille
15g egg whites
25g icing sugar
20g butter
20g plain flour
½ vanilla bean
3 lime segments, pith and pips removed

Bring the sugar and 100ml water to the boil, stirring to ensure the sugar is dissolved. Remove from heat and add the lime juice.

Blanch the zest 3 times in boiling water, refreshing between each time, and then place in the syrup.

Stir well and refrigerate.

In a small saucepan, combine the cream and liquorice and heat gently, without boiling, until the liquorice is very soft. Blend the mixture in a food processor until well combined and pour through a fine sieve to strain out the tiny pieces of liquorice. Set aside to cool.

In a stainless steel bowl over a large saucepan of gently simmering water, make a sabayon by whisking together the eggs, yolk, glucose, sugar and Pernod until the mixture turns pale and fluffy. Remove from heat and continue whisking until it cools a little. Fold half of the sabayon into the liquorice mixture. Once combined, fold in the remaining sabayon until well combined. Pour into individual dariole moulds, or in 1 log shaped-tin, and freeze.

Place all tuille ingredients in the food processor and blend for 4–5 minutes until smooth. Rest for one hour before using. Using a pastry card and circle template, scrape the mixture onto greaseproof paper and put in the oven with weights on the corners. Remove from the oven and wrap around wooden spoon handle while still warm to form a cigar shape.

To serve, lower the moulds into hot water for a few seconds before turning out the parfait. You can either pour over the lime syrup or serve it on the table in a jug. Garnish with lime segments.

Tart of Sesame Grilled Rabbit, Creamy Polenta, Shiitake Mushrooms

Serves 4

Short Pastry (makes 10 tartlets)
60g butter
Pinch salt
100g flour
1 egg
Milk, to moisten
Pinch sugar

Polenta
2 cups milk
200g medium grain polenta
50ml cream
Salt
100g Grana Padano (Parmesan)

4 rabbit fillets
1 teaspoon soy
1 teaspoon sesame oil
¼ punnet shiitake mushrooms
1 knob ginger
Chives (finely chopped)

Place butter, flour, salt and sugar in a food processor. Add egg and milk until it combines to become a ball. Knead pastry for a few minutes then rest for 30 minutes.

Once rested, roll out pastry and stamp out with a round cutter. Press into pastry mould and blind bake at 180°C for 8 minutes.

Bring milk to boil. Slowly whisk in polenta and cook for about 45 minutes to an hour. The grain should be just cooked. Add cream, salt and Parmesan. Set aside in a bain marie to stay warm.

Marinade rabbit fillet with soy and sesame oil for about an hour. Set aside a quarter of the shiitake mushrooms.

Chargrill rabbit for 2–5 minutes. Rest. Spoon polenta into pastry case. Slice rabbit to go around tartlet. Reheat mushrooms and place on top. Drizzle with jus infused with ginger. Sprinkle with chives.

16

CARDS DEALT TO SINGLE DINERS

I've always considered myself pretty lucky. Perhaps it's a combination of the luck of the Irish and growing up in the lucky country, I'm not sure, but during one trip to the USA in the lead up to the opening of my very first restaurant, Lady Luck once again shined on me and changed some of my perceptions of dining forever.

I'd lasted four years in my first real head chef position and Lucy and I had a thorough understanding of how to run a successful business, but we'd never owned our very own restaurant. So in the downtime between CBD and the start of our new venture I decided to travel to the USA for a week-long journey. I wanted to get inspired by taking a first-hand look at the way some of the best restaurants in the Big Apple did their thing.

First stop: Las Vegas.

If you've never been, it's something I'd urge anyone to experience. It's arguably the craziest town on the planet and a hell of a lot of fun to boot. You have this bizarre cocktail of millionaires and buxom beauties, dancers and daredevils, impersonators, party animals, career gamblers, destroyed gamblers and a few freaks and fashionistas too. All of whom radiate under the plastic promise of the neon lights... ah, viva Las Vegas.

From the moment you arrive you get this overwhelming sense of excitement, with a touch of fear. Mostly, you thrive on the opportunity to fill your pockets and enjoy the moment.

I've always been a bit of a punter. It's almost a rite of passage for young males in Australia to have a bit of a gamble, try your luck and have a bit of a laugh along the way. If you need convincing of its place in Australia's social construct just take a look at ANZAC day and our two-up ritual, or The Melbourne Cup. It's quite obvious that it's heavily ingrained in our culture. So here I was, in the bright lights of Vegas. When I go into a casino, there's really only one game for me: blackjack. I found a dealer who I liked the look of. You know the type: the one who looks like they're going to deal you a run of good cards. Some might call it superstitious but I just go on a feeling. It's also a hell of a lot more fun if it's a female dealer, because it's nice to have a laugh along the way as well. For me there is only one way to play, and that's one on one. It cuts out the stupid play of those who don't know the game and means I'm in control of the situation as much as possible. The last thing you want is to have a decent hand and some muppet sitting at the end of the table takes the dealer's card and prevents you from winning.

So I pulled up a chair and put US$1000 on the line. Sounds huge, and at that time in my life US$1000, was a pretty big outlay, but I thought *hey, what the hell, I'm in Vegas, so why the hell not roll the dice and see what comes of it.* I've always believed that fortune favours the brave.

The first hour was just a lot of fun and I neither lost or gained any money, but then within a very short space I got on a run. I had managed to work up a pretty big stack of chips and decided to push my luck with a big punt. I anted up $1000. What the hell was I thinking? My heart went into over-drive pounding against my chest and my stomach churned through fear and anticipation. First card hit the table: the eight of hearts. Second card lands: the eight of spades. The dealer had a four of diamonds on show. The only smart thing to do with a pair like that is split them. But that meant another $1000 onto the table. Ouch. I thought this could be my chance, so I did it. I split the two eights and hoped to God that my next cards were on the money. There was $2000 riding on it!

The dealer dealt my first card onto the eight of hearts: the three of spades. Total eleven. Do I double down? If I double down it meant I could get 21, but it also meant I had to throw another $1000 in. What was I thinking? I thought, fuck it, how often do you get to go to Vegas? So I doubled down, and the card hit the table. The nine of hearts. That meant one of my hands totalled 20 and there was $2000 riding on it. Stand. Now to my other hand. I had my other eight with $1000 on it. It was insane! The dealer hit it. A Jack of clubs! You beauty! I had two hands, one hand of 18 with $1000 on the line and the other a 20 with $2000. Talk about sweating bullets. I was shitting myself, but that nervous energy of chance is intoxicating. So I had a total of $3000 on the line but I had two great hands that could very easily turn to dust if the dealer pulled a rabbit out of her... hat!

'Two good hands Sir, good luck, dealer has a four,' she said.

Then bang, the dealer turns her card over. The King of Clubs. Argh! I couldn't sit still. The agony, *just get on with it!* I thought!

'Dealer has fourteen, not enough, another card,' she said as she flipped the next card.

A three of diamonds!

'Dealer has 17, congratulations Sir,' she said.

Come on! I couldn't believe it. I'd just won $3000 in the space of three minutes. It might just be the biggest fucking grin that's ever appeared on my face.

That took me into the stratosphere, so I had one or two more normal bets to calm my excitement. While I knew I was well ahead, I wasn't sure exactly where I was money-wise, so I decided to do a chip count. I nearly fell off my chair. Holy shit, I'd converted US$1000 into US$10,000. Talk about lucky. To be honest I've probably lost three times that amount by now, but never mind. At that time I felt like a bloody millionaire.

So here I was in Vegas, about to go on a fact finding food tour of New York, and all of a sudden I had $10k spending money. I thanked the dealer, pushed in my chair and pulled up stumps. New York beckoned.

The next morning I woke up and I still couldn't wipe the huge grin off my face. I flew to New York and over the next four days blew the whole $10K indulging myself in some of the finest examples of top shelf restaurateuring on the planet.

I stayed at the luxurious boutique Mercer Hotel in Soho. It's in a wonderful old Romanesque building with 70-odd loft apartments, and it truly made me feel like a king. It is the hotel made famous by a phone-throwing Russell Crowe!

Every day I donned one of my best suits, tie and all. Nowadays I can't stand wearing a tie. I'm not even sure why I wore one then, I guess I was trying to play the part and live the dream. Over four days I must have gained about five kilos because I ate at the best restaurants for lunch, dinner, lunch, dinner, lunch, dinner, lunch and finally dinner. A table for one, every single time.

I had a notebook on the table and I took notes. I drank the best wine, ate the most amazing food and it was an incredible awakening for me to watch how restaurateurs and their staff run different establishments. I was just inhaling it all: sucking in as much information and experience as I could.

I made my way through a procession of wonderful restaurants including Balthazar, a classic and thriving bistro started by Keith McNally back in 1997. The place oozed energy and the food was right on the money of what you'd expect from a traditional French bistro. I went to Jean-Georges in the Trump International Hotel and Tower, the landmark establishment of three-Michelin-star chef Jean-Georges Vongerichten. Two Danny Meyer restaurants, Gramercy Tavern, one of my all-time true American favourites, and Tabla Restaurant also made the list. But the best experience for me was lunch at Bouley Bakery. The little 20-odd seater was the creation of David Bouley; however, sadly, is no longer there in the form that enthralled me.

I got all dressed up again, put on the suit and tie looking like a pseudo-million dollar man and arrived at Bouley Bakery for a table for one at 2pm.

The place was full, and granted, it only seated about 20 people so that wasn't hard, but the quaint space felt welcoming and buzzed with an energy of comfortable confidence within itself. The waiter politely took me to my table and I said 'Can the chef just cook for me, and you match it with the wines you think work best and charge me what you think is right?'

He happily obliged.

It's a very bold statement. Just feed me and quench my thirst. It's a gamble, because you have no idea what the bill will be at the end, but I always feel it's a great opportunity for the chef to show someone what they can do. I love it when I'm given the challenge. If a diner ever comes in and says 'just cook for me', I take it as a wonderful opportunity to show off and dish up what I do best.

I love the adventure of it: the anticipation of what might come next. You end up getting a thorough understanding of a chef's cooking philosophy when you leave the journey in their hands.

So I was sitting with my little notepad scribbling notes for myself. Here's this funny looking fellow in a suit and tie who's asked for a food and wine journey and he's writing notes at every opportunity, and like many restaurant critics that I've seen come and go, he's dining alone. Perhaps they thought I was a food critic? I guess I'll never know.

From the minute the waiter walked over with the bread trolley to the minute I left the restaurant—with a loaf of my favourite bread under my arm, mind you—it was simply unbelievable. It was quite possibly one of the best meals I have ever had, and it wasn't just about the food. I arrived at Bouley Bakery at 2pm and left at 6:30pm. Now, I've had some long lunches in my time, but for a single diner that takes the cake. Four and a half hours, and the whole time I never felt awkward, never felt like an inconvenience or out of place, which unfortunately I think happens to a lot of single diners. By the end of it, I'd spoken to every waiter, met the chefs and felt so welcomed. I'd just had the best time you could imagine.

The award-winning crew from Salt. On the left is Darren 'Daggy' Barnett.
On chair front left is head chef Mark Holmes, and next to me
on the chair holding an award is Lucy Allon.

In Melbourne at the Flowerdrum with the geezer Jamie Oliver.

My main men during 2003. Shannon Binnie, Perry Hill and Mark Holmes on the balcony of Moorish.

With my great mate Chris Lynch. Can't believe we've been best mates for 30 years!

Special dinner for Hermann Schneider at Grossi Florentino in 2004. (L-R) John Lepp, Hermann Schneider, Guy's sister Elizabeth, Guy Grossi, Faye Schneider, mum (Marie Mangan) and me.

Judging the Electrolux Young Chef of the Year 2010 program. The calibre of young chefs these days is amazing.

Judging the Electrolux Young Chef 2010 award. Clockwise from left: Guy Grossi, Anthony Musarra, me, Peter Doyle, Tetsuya Wakuda and Lyndey Milan. (Adrian Lander Photography)

Helping Paul Bocuse judge the Australian representative for the Bocuse d'Or 2007.

With Joe Pavlovich in my Sydney restaurant glass.
(Photograph courtesy of glass brasserie)

With Former US President Bill Clinton. It was an honour to cook for the great man.

At a G'day USA event in New York and LA 2008, with fellow Aussie chef Neil Perry and my good mate Richard 'Dickie' Wilkins.

A signed album cover from Chris Isaak. I was so excited to have dinner with him in the USA!

Merry Christmas

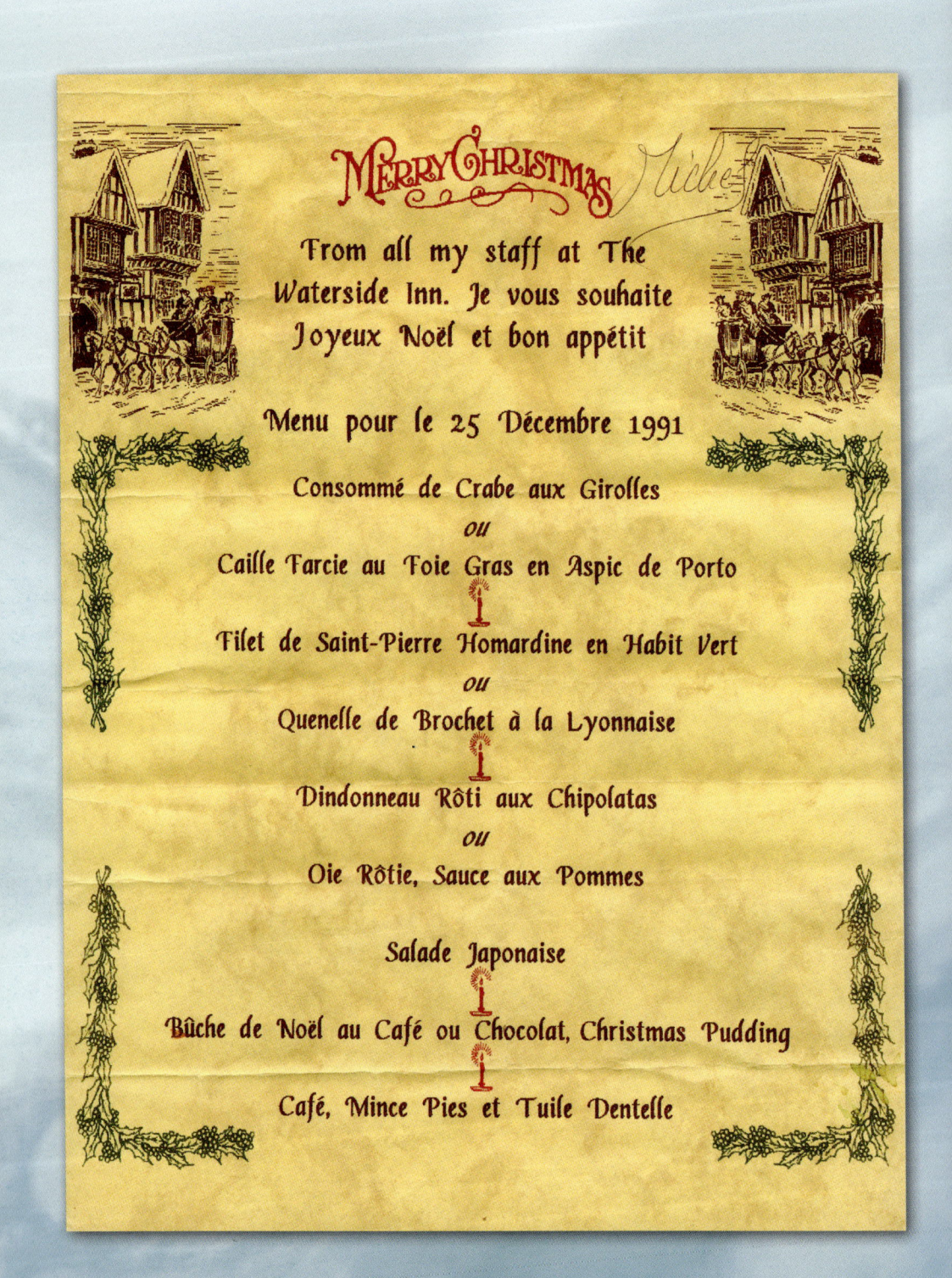

From all my staff at The Waterside Inn. Je vous souhaite Joyeux Noël et bon appétit

Menu pour le 25 Décembre 1991

Consommé de Crabe aux Girolles

ou

Caille Farcie au Foie Gras en Aspic de Porto

Filet de Saint-Pierre Homardine en Habit Vert

ou

Quenelle de Brochet à la Lyonnaise

Dindonneau Rôti aux Chipolatas

ou

Oie Rôtie, Sauce aux Pommes

Salade Japonaise

Bûche de Noël au Café ou Chocolat, Christmas Pudding

Café, Mince Pies et Tuile Dentelle

Christmas menu from The Waterside Inn! Sounds delicious!

That trip to all those restaurants, especially Bouley Bakery, made me realise what it's truly like to be a single diner. One thing you can say about American restaurants: their waiters really know customer service. I know they work for tips, but they've got the service side of things down pat. It dawned on me in those four days that you really have to look after single diners: they are very, very important. A lot of restaurants make the mistake of rushing a single diner through the experience to get them out of the restaurant as if they are some sort of awkward adolescent covered in pimples, sticking out like an eyesore among the cool crowd.

It's a huge error on the part of any restaurant to dismiss the importance of a single diner. You really have no idea who that single diner is. They could be a restaurant critic, they could be a traveller, they could be a businessman who comes to your town for two days out of every week, or they could simply be someone who enjoys food and new experiences.

The reality is that a single diner is someone who has made a hell of an effort to come to your establishment to eat. Think about it. When you go out to dine with other people often there's a reason like catching up with friends, a celebration, a business meeting, it could be anything. But a single diner has made the decision on their own to be there. They need to eat and they've decided that although they are eating alone they are happy to travel all the way to your establishment for the food and the experience.

Everyone's money is the same colour, and who knows, that person might come back once a week for a year if you've given them a reason to. More often than not they will bring a group of friends next time. Those friends might individually bring another four friends the time after. You can do the maths from here on. It's practically business

CARDS DEALT TO SINGLE DINERS

suicide to neglect any guest at your establishment, and for me single diners are the last client you should be dismissing as a thorn in your side.

It's a big thing for me in my restaurants. I tell my staff 'you have to look after the single diners.' Think about it as if you were sitting there by yourself having dinner, and how you would like to be treated. Give them a newspaper, ask them if they want anything... perhaps a conversation if they seem interested, or even give them a tour of the kitchen. Something out of the ordinary to make that experience personal and memorable. If you release that awkwardness some associate with single diners by making them feel as welcome as any other person who comes to eat at your establishment you'll win a client for life. Perception is everything in the hospitality industry and a positive experience, one where restaurant staff have gone the extra yard to make someone's night, won't be forgotten.

Bouley Bakery did that for me.

17

TURNING SAUSAGES INTO SALT

We left CBD in December 1997. We had no idea what our next gig was going to be but Lucy and I were keen to start our own restaurant. As we scoured the city for potential sites we needed to get in a steady income to help pay the bills and put food on the plate.

I'd had some experience making sausages in all the restaurants I'd worked in, but in 1997 I was hired by Barry McDonald to create a Federation beef sausage for sale in the retail market. Federation beef was one of the first marble-scored beefs to come into Australia, and we used it at CBD. It was wonderful beef. The sausages we created were unreal, and we used Irish skins made from dried natural intestines. The flavour was amazing—it was almost like eating a steak!

That experience gave me an idea. I started my own line of sausages to bridge that gap between CBD and our next project. They had the grower's markets down in Pyrmont in Sydney on a Saturday morning, so I started off selling them down there in a stall.

The brand was called Sausages by Luke Mangan. It was the first insight I had into the power behind marketing a food product as a brand. We sold them for $5 and for that you'd get a snag, caramelised onion and a bun. I'd sell 400–500 in a morning, giddy up! We'd have our own homemade barbecue sauce for sale on the side as well.

We promoted the Sausages by Luke Mangan as 'All meat, no fat, no preservatives', and we'd say to every one of our customers 'don't prick your sausages, you'll let all the juices out!'

We did four types: chicken and tarragon, beef and marjoram, lamb and mint, and pork and sage. They got pretty popular, and I couldn't believe the amount of press we were getting for a bunch of sausages. We were making them out of a factory in Riverstone. I'd wake up at 5:30am and, with another guy, would drive out to Riverstone and spend all morning making sausages.

We were selling about 1000 kilograms of sausages a week. It turned out to be a good little business, and when we added the spicy homemade barbecue sauce and got it into David Jones and delis, I was making $2-3K a week, it was insane. Nice way to supplement your income while looking for a new restaurant site!

Although the mornings were taken up by handling a hell of a lot of sausages, the afternoons were all about finding a site to live out the dream of opening our own restaurant.

LUKE MANGAN

There was this place opposite the Intercontinental down in Circular Quay that we took a look at too. It was, and still is, an Indian Restaurant called Karma. I think the name put us off that site.

We were also approached by the people who owned the Astor building on Macquarie Street. In its day it was quite famous and there was a restaurant in the basement, so we looked at that as well. Again we weren't a hundred per cent sure.

We didn't know where our next restaurant was going to be or even exactly what it was going to be like. It is similar to when you are going to look for a house; it is not until you walk in the door and see it that you think, *yep, this is exactly what I want.*

We got in touch with a mate of mine called Don Petroff, who was the kitchen guy from Austmont kitchens. He had done our kitchen at CBD, and he advised us that there was a new 40-room boutique hotel going up in Darlinghurst, The Kirketon Hotel, and he said I should meet the guys who owned the building.

Owners Robert and Terry Schwamberg were putting the pieces together of this beautiful new boutique hotel, designed by Iain Halliday, and they were on the lookout for a restaurant operator to capture the imagination of the dining public with a great restaurant and bar.

We met with them and they told us they were talking to two or three other people to see if their visions for the place were on the same page, but they seemed really keen for us to go into it.

Lucy and I had a great vibe on the project from the outset, but it was a major decision for us to make. We were still young and it was a substantial investment. They really pushed us for an answer. So we pulled back, wanting to take our time thinking about it because it was such a big commitment. We had to make sure whatever decision we made that it was the right one for us. The project was still in the build stage and wouldn't be due to open until February 1999.

The Schwambergs wanted to see the right operator in there. They were savvy enough to realise that the food element would be a major drawcard for a boutique hotel in the city. After the success and favourable media with CBD they were very keen, but we realised we simply didn't have the money that they wanted us to invest into it.

We walked away a bit disappointed, and so did they, but the Schwambergs weren't done yet.

Robert rang me and said 'Look, come over for dinner and we'll discuss it. Terry and I really want to make it happen, so let's see if we can make it happen.'

Over dinner they floated the idea that they would offer a rent-free period which would assist us into the project. They were great to give us this start but they knew what they would get out of it at the same time. This was very attractive because we'd looked at a lot places that were set up, and pretty much all of them needed a lot of money re-invested to get them to the level we wanted. The plus on this build was that we were potentially early enough into it that we could actually decide how we wanted things to be laid out in the kitchen. That was a real deal clincher.

So we put our house in Paddington on the market, went into overdrive making sausages and saved like hell.

The property market was going through a strong period and was on the up. Although we'd only had our house for about eight months, and had bought for $285,000, we sold it at auction for $400,000. A profit of $115,000. It was crazy. The house was just a simple two-up, two-down terrace, with a really narrow tiny back garden that ran onto a central laneway at the back. We did absolutely nothing to it, we rented it out for the whole time we owned it. It felt like we'd won the lottery at sale.

We invested all of our sausage money plus the profits from our house and everything else we could scrape together in the restaurant. It was game on, and we had the full attention of the media penning our every move.

Obviously the Schwambergs had employed designer Iain Halliday for the whole hotel, so we had to fit in with the design in that respect. Iain did this amazing, slick, modern restaurant with a stunning lavender wall feature that was just beautiful. But I planned the whole kitchen, which was pretty cool. It's what you want as a head chef: to design and build the kitchen from scratch. It allows you to create maximum efficiency within the space according to the way you cook and run your team.

Lucy and I planned everything, from the chairs down to the napery, crockery and cutlery. I remember when we put the deposit down for the chairs, we almost fell off ours! The deposit alone was $35,000. We imported 140 chairs from Italy that were about $400 each, which works out at about $56,000 just for bloody chairs!

We completely underestimated how hard it is to run a restaurant, especially the business side of things. Even though we ran the restaurant at CBD, it's different when it's actually your own business. This time it was our money and the experience was very nerve wracking. You monitor every cent you spend and you have to make some pretty tough decisions on where the money is best spent. It's a challenge. There are always things that you want but you just can't afford. So you hold back on certain things and splash out on the important elements that will make your business work.

TURNING SAUSAGES INTO SALT

We made the investment in things like chairs, but we got cheap tables made and had backing and soundproofing made for them, because we knew we'd double-cloth them anyway.

It was frantic, every day. I don't think we really understood the gravity of what we had gotten ourselves into. We were still on the high of having an opportunity, but as each day went by the realisation of getting everything right and making it a success was starting to hit home. It had to work or we were going to lose all the money we invested, which was everything we had. Even worse, perhaps we'd lose our good reputations as well. Failure wasn't an option.

We were nearly a hundred per cent complete on the build, and we still hadn't agreed on a name for the restaurant. The early favourite was Alchemy, the notion of turning base metals into gold, and the twist to it with what we would do with produce in the kitchen, turning basic produce into gold. The defining restaurant in my career could have been named Alchemy, and in hindsight I'm glad it wasn't. I've often wondered if it would have had the same appeal.

We got a few friends together, Eric and Rachael. They loved the restaurant and we thought they were the right guys to be involved in creating a name. We brainstormed about 100 different names for our very first restaurant and it came back to a simple and honest idea, much like our approach to food and dining. One name just kept popping up: Salt.

Back in ancient Greek days, salt was a rare and expensive commodity, and it was given to people as a sign of hospitality and friendship. We wanted our restaurant to be both hospitable and friendly. You can't cook without salt and it's vital to the balance of a dish.

And so, Salt was born. The name of the wine and cigar bar was a simple flow-on effect: Fix. Everyone needs their salt fix.

18

STRIKING GOLD IN THE SALT MINES

Salt had a turnover of $5.9 million in its first year of trade. We were named the Best New Restaurant in the *Sydney Morning Herald Good Food Guide* 2000 and given the status of two chef's hats with a score of 17/20.

It was an astounding year for Lucy and I, and the whole Salt team. We'd worked our arses off and our dream of having our very own successful restaurant was well and truly being realised.

We had a great team. In the kitchen I had my crew from CBD, Mark Holmes as my head chef, and Shannon Binnie, who was now qualified. Lucy had her front of house team firing on all cylinders, which included my good mate Darren Barnett as sommelier.

STRIKING GOLD IN THE SALT MINES

I was 28/29, and I had something to prove. Getting those awards was really important to me, personally and professionally. Nowadays, although accolades are nice if they come my way, they aren't the be all and end all. It's ultimately not what pays the bills: hard work pays the bills.

Salt was a step forwards for me, creatively speaking. CBD allowed me to test the waters, but Salt let me come into my own. If CBD was an incarnation of Kensington Place, then Salt was my interpretation of what I experienced at The Waterside Inn.

I felt it was time to take it up a notch from what we achieved at CBD. It was the way I liked to cook and the way I like to eat, with a touch of magic. Keep it simple, full of flavour, let the key ingredients speak for themselves and don't overcomplicate it.

Some of my favourite dishes on the menu at Salt included tempura quail, wasabi dipping sauce, carrot and diakon, or the sashimi salmon with ginger soy and shallot dressing and the roasted barramundi with preserved lemon and basil risotto and sweet pea sauce. Sure, these dishes sound busy, but they were stripped back and simple on the plate. I think that's what defined Salt.

Truth be known, I didn't want Salt to be fine dining; I wanted it to be formal but friendly, not stuffy. We still wanted to retain that brasserie style and we didn't want a hushed dining space, we wanted it to be an extra nice drop-in place where people can go when they're a bit hungry. And that's what we ended up with.

There's no doubt that all the accolades had a huge effect on the business though. The hard thing about winning those awards is you get people coming in who have never dined with you before, with all these high expectations—preconceived expectations—before they've even entered the building.

LUKE MANGAN

We were busy already, but winning the Best New Restaurant award made it even busier and the dynamic changed. We still had our regulars, but a new crowd came in wanting to see what all the fuss was about. One thing I've learned is once your review is on paper in black and white, a lot of consumers will compare their experience of dining at your restaurant to the critic's column. The reality is the critic's column is just one person's opinion.

For me, Terry Durack had great power back then, as he does now, and he is one of the few truly respected food critics who has the 'real experience' to judge. That makes the challenge of pleasing him even more fun.

Don't get me wrong, we wanted the accolades and were very happy about achieving them, and from the publicity point of view it keeps you out there in the media too. It just opens up a whole new world once the review hits the paper. To be fair, the media focus on Salt was nothing short of stupendously positive in the early years, and it had a major impact on things to come.

And dealing with a new and interesting clientele was the least of our worries.

Our first laundry bill was five fucking thousand dollars for the month. We didn't think of things like that. We just never thought of the breakage of glassware or crockery, or the cutlery that mysteriously goes missing, or staff who give free drinks away to their friends. You just don't consider those sort of costs. You are aware of them, but until Salt we never had to pay them ourselves with our own money, and that's where it became different.

The problem was, we opened the doors before we really had a proper business plan. We knew what we wanted to achieve, but it certainly wasn't put together as a proper formal plan as I would do

STRIKING GOLD IN THE SALT MINES

now. That's the beauty of being young: you are more willing to take the risk. But for anyone now who wants to start up a business, I'd encourage you to have a proper plan in place.

We opened the doors and put everything on the line. If it failed who knows where we would be. But it was the best experience ever, and the biggest learning curve for both Lucy and me.

We were busier than we had ever envisaged and all of the media attention was getting us noticed abroad.

I guess Salt was a very sophisticated restaurant for that time in Australia. In our second year it was very difficult to get into and it seemed like every second table was taken up by someone of wealth or fame. At times I wasn't quite sure of the best way to deal with some of them, I mean what would I know about celebrities? I was just a bloody chef!

I'd become great friends with food journalist and wine lover Guy Griffin in the later years of CBD. He'd written a glowing review of the restaurant and through numerous visits he'd befriended Lucy, and it wasn't long before Guy and I shared a meal and a wine and it was obvious to both of us we had a lot in common. Ever since we've been great mates.

As Salt's popularity snowballed and we became a den for wannabes, the wannabe seen and the rarely seen, I'd call on Guy when we had international food journalists in the restaurant so he could help host them and give them a great picture of the Australian food scene.

On one particular night I rang Guy. He was writing for *Australian Gourmet Traveller* at the time and was on his way home from work. I said 'there's a deeply tanned guy in a white suit sitting at the bar with a gorgeous blonde. He says his name is Adrian Gill, apparently he's a famous food writer in the UK. Do you want to come in and meet him, and say "hi"?'

LUKE MANGAN

It was, of course, none other than British restaurant critic AA Gill sitting in Fix cigar and wine bar with a lady named Nicola Formby, who would eventually become his long-term partner. I had no idea who he was. Of course Guy did. 'Are you kidding me? I'm on my way there now,' came his reply. And thankfully after his visit Adrian gave Salt a glowing review

Adrian and Guy hit it off immediately.

AA Gill wasn't the only interesting character to wander through the doors at Salt. One Easter, we'd finished the Sunday lunch service, and since the restaurant was shut Sunday nights we decided to have a special dinner just for the staff. At about 6pm the phone rang, and I got up from my chair. 'Hi, this is Salt, how can I help you?'

This female voice on the other side of the phone asked 'Are you open tonight? Jamie Oliver would like to come in for dinner.'

I said 'Oh, look it's Sunday night. We're actually closed.'

The voice on the other end of the line said 'But it's Jamie Oliver, and he really wants to come in for dinner tonight.'

I had no idea who he was. So I said 'Can you hold the line for a second?' I put her on hold and asked out loud, 'Has anyone heard of a Jamie Oliver?'

One of my staff replied, 'yeah, he's an English chef that's on TV and has his own show over there.'

So I got back on the phone and said 'We aren't actually open, but we are having a staff Easter dinner. He is most welcome to come along and join us.'

So Jamie came along for our staff dinner. We formed a good friendship for the next few years, and he even came out to Australia and cooked at Salt. It was my 30th birthday at the time so we had a bit of a night out, we were living large!

STRIKING GOLD IN THE SALT MINES

For a period Salt was the hottest place to be. On any given night we'd have celebrities like Susan Sarandon, Tom Cruise, Nicole Kidman, Michel Roux or even Richard Branson in the restaurant. The place was out of control. Of course I never saw any of it: we were too busy pumping out the food in the kitchen. Even the floor staff were just too busy to get carried away with the profile of some of our clientele.

I remember one night Baz Luhrmann and Lachlan Murdoch were sitting on table 12 at the front window of the restaurant enjoying dinner when a Jeep Wrangler lost control, flipped onto its roof and came up onto the pavement. It almost came in through the front window of the restaurant. We all froze for a moment and feared the worst. Thankfully it came to a halt before the window. No doubt Baz and Lachlan's lives flashed before their eyes. The incident even made headlines in the papers. We still enjoy the pleasure of Baz's company these days at glass brasserie, he's been a wonderful supporter of what we do.

On the back of the success of Salt my media profile was going into overdrive. I was appearing on television both here and, thanks to the Sydney Olympics, in the USA as well. A friend at the time knew one of the producers for the NBC *Today* shows, and I was chosen to cook on the *Today Morning Show*, which was beamed live from the Olympic village into the living rooms of residents back in the States. It helped forge a relationship with Katie Couric and Matt Lauer that has seen me appear on their show every year since.

In that first year of Salt I also released my very first cookbook, *BLD: Breakfast, Lunch and Dinner*. Lisa Hudson, a journalist friend

LUKE MANGAN

from Fairfax, worked tirelessly with me on that project and the first print run sold out.

I've released four books in total to date, including *BLD* (1999), *Luke Mangan Food* (2002), then *Luke Mangan Classics* (2004) and *Luke Mangan at Home and in the Mood* (2009) with New Holland.

The great thing about releasing a cookbook is that it can open doors for you. Thanks to the release of my first book, I did my first cooking segment on Nine Network's *Today Show* with Tracy Grimshaw in about 2000. She was hosting the program with Steve Liebmann in those days, and I think I only got the gig because I was promoting *BLD* at the time.

We had a real good time doing that, and I think Tracy had a lot to do with the push to have me on as a regular. Tracy and I got on really well and we had a real ball cooking over the years. I ended up being the *Today Show* food editor for about eight years, which is incredible for my brand. One of the most watched shows on morning television and I scored a regular cooking spot! It was unreal.

One morning Chris Isaak was on the *Today Show*. I ended up doing the cooking segment with a good mate of mine, Richard 'Dicky' Wilkins, and Chris Isaak. It was a blast, especially because I've always loved his music. And believe what you read: Chris is one hell of a cool cat. The ladies go weak at the knees for him.

As it so happened, a few years later I was in the USA doing a cooking segment on the *Morning Show* on Fox LA, and Chris Isaak was on after my cooking segment. We got chatting backstage and he said 'Hey, let's go out for dinner tonight while you're in LA.'

I thought *wow, how cool is that, dinner with Chris Isaak!* So I said 'Let's go to Mario Batali's restaurant Mozza, he's a mate of mine.' So it was set.

Later that day Chris rang me and said 'Do you mind if I bring some people with me?' I said 'yeah no worries', so I rang Mario and increased the numbers booked.

I met Chris and his manager Sheryl at the restaurant. We were sitting at the bar having a drink waiting for the other guests to arrive and in walked Michael Bublé with two older people. The whole room watched him walk in, as they had when Chris walked in because he'd just released his new album that was going gangbusters.

People started whispering 'Hey it's Michael Bublé,' and then he walked up to us and Chris introduced me to him! It turned out he was our dining companion, and he'd brought his parents along with him.

I couldn't believe it. Dinner with Chris Isaak and Michael Bublé. Was this all a dream?

19

THE EMPIRE EXPANDS

Lucy and I split up just over a year into Salt. No one knew except us, and we tried to get on with business as usual. We are both very stubborn people. It was tense at times, but we managed to keep it a secret from staff for a considerable amount of time.

We both felt very emotionally attached to the personal investment we had made into Salt: all the blood, sweat and tears. We knew we were fantastic as a team and had made the restaurant successful. Neither of us wanted to let it go.

The advantage we had at Salt was Lucy was a restaurant owner on the floor and I was a restaurant owner in the kitchen. Both bases were covered to a certain degree. Neither of us even raised the notion of selling the business, we just got on with it.

THE EMPIRE EXPANDS

Working together and living together in that environment isn't easy. When we opened Salt we lived in the hotel upstairs for the first three months. Two people living in a hotel room, and heading downstairs to work all day and night... it was just too much. To Lucy's credit, she is a workhorse. She is more rational than me: she thinks about things first, whereas I just do things and can have a bit of a hot head. She handled things very well, but we were both putting in 100 hours and living in a shoebox. We were just in each other's face too much. I'd be in the kitchen yelling and screaming all day, and I probably directed blame at Lucy and the floor staff for years on end in the heat of service.

In hindsight, either Lucy or I should have walked away from Salt once we broke up. But both of us had so much invested into it that neither of us wanted to do that. So we just got on with it and basically became business partners.

Strangely, not only did we continue working together making Salt a success, we added to our restaurant portfolio, not once, but twice more.

Salt was booming, the Olympics had put a spotlight on Australian tourism and food and the whole city was vibrant and full of opportunity. I wanted to open a new restaurant, something more casual, like a classic French bistro. We looked at a site in Sydney's Taylor Square, of all places. It was right across the road from Kinsellas—once made famous by Tony Bilson—but we didn't go ahead with the deal.

At that time a great friend of mine, Barry McDonald, was supplying our veg and I told him I wanted to do a French bistro. He had interest in La Mensa in Paddington with Steve Manfredi at the time, but wanted to change the concept. He said 'Why don't you do it there?'

So I spoke to Lucy, and we all agreed it was a great opportunity.

Barry introduced us to a guy called Simon Mordant, who's become a great mate and someone I trust to bounce ideas off still. He was keen to invest as well, so we had two partners in the project.

It meant we were given the opportunity to do something more casual than Salt. It was exciting. Salt was great, but it had become quite fine dining and particular in its style. We both yearned for the chance to do something in that brasserie style again: relaxed, casual and heart-warming.

Suddenly it was all happening. I think we were the only business in Sydney that closed during the Olympics. We were working on changing from the old La Mensa concept to this new one, so we thought while everyone is going crazy we'll just quietly close the doors, do what we need to do and reopen after the Olympics.

We named it Bistro Lulu: the Lulu meaning 'Lu' from Luke and 'Lu' from Lucy.

The room had a Parisian feel about it: stripped back and bare. No white linen tablecloths: instead we had aged bentwood chairs, wood panelling, mirrored panels and banquettes along the main wall. We were on a shoestring budget, and a friend of Barry's, Neil Bradford, helped us with the interior design and did a wonderful job of taking it all back to basics.

The brief in the kitchen was 'keep it simple and have bags of flavour'. We had the classics like French onion soup with gruyere crouton; steak, frites and café de Paris butter; chicken liver parfait with pickled red cabbage; and a simple banana tarte tartin.

We had a great team. Alastair Smith was appointed head chef and Annie Lundin ran the front of house. In our first year we were awarded a *Sydney Morning Herald Good Food Guide* chef's hat, and chief critic Matthew Evans gave us a 15/20 in a glowing review. We

THE EMPIRE EXPANDS

were rapt with the press Lulu was receiving. Things were going just as we'd planned.

Sadly, about a year after Lulu opened, Alastair Smith had a really bad motorcycle accident on his way home from work. In fact it was so bad he was lucky it didn't kill him. It meant he was off work for one to two years of rehabilitation. It was horrendous for the guy, but we left his position open for as long as we could, and it got to a stage where his rehabilitation wasn't getting any better over those two years. Alastair found it hard to get back in the kitchen, but I hear he's cheffing again these days, which is nice.

I obviously had to appoint someone to be head chef at Lulu in Alastair's absence. We had this young hungry chef who had only just joined us: Joe Pavlovich. We appointed him as a temporary head chef until we knew what was happening with Al.

Joe did a great job, just as Al had, and took Lulu to a new level with a mix of his enthusiasm and understanding of the brief: keep it simple. Joe understood what I wanted to a T. The way I like to do things is to give the chefs a base menu, and then let them play around with the specials and come up with new ideas. So we'd work together on the menu at Lulu. Once I trust the chef, my philosophy is to give them as much freedom as I can, otherwise they just piss off somewhere else. Giving chefs that freedom shows your belief in them and creates respect. It also gives them a sense of ownership over what happens in the kitchen.

That sort of system has been a huge ingredient in the recipe of my success. I'm a firm believer of promoting from within the company if it is possible rather than getting in expertise. I already know the strengths and weaknesses of my staff, and I'd rather promote someone I know rather than employ a person I know little or nothing about.

LUKE MANGAN

That sends a clear message to the staff that they have a future with us, and as we are growing there will be opportunities. It promotes loyal staff who believe in, and are passionate about, your product.

Salt and Lulu were powering along nicely when a bloke who was involved in several restaurants approached Lucy and I about a possible project in North Bondi, practically on the beach under the North Bondi RSL. It was a dream location for any operator.

With everything going so well with our businesses we were all ears for what looked like a no-brainer for success.

Our partner was essentially the moneyman, but the business arrangement would be a little different than what we were used to. We owned Salt and Lulu, but Moorish was a consulting management deal with a small ownership. As part of our management deal we received a monthly fee. Essentially our partner was in charge of raising the money and getting investors and we did what we did. We hired the staff, designed the restaurant and menu and ran the day-to-day business.

We wanted to do something that did not compete with what our other restaurants did. There's absolutely no point in competing against yourself in business. Lucy and I had always loved Moroccan food, and being a stone's throw from the sandy beach at Bondi we thought, what better cuisine to have in the sun? The design was deliberately simple to put the total focus on the sweeping views of Bondi Beach. When you have a view like that the décor is practically irrelevant.

It was a great business and it was on fire really from the moment the doors were flung open in 2003. We put Perry Hill in charge of the kitchen. He'd worked at CBD, Salt and Lulu and was ideally suited for the brief at Moorish. Perry is a great chef, and since working with us went on to weave his magic at The Boathouse on Blackwattle Bay before heading north to The Point Bar and Restaurant in Ballina.

The menu was rustically robust with dishes like braised lamb shoulder with dried figs, black olives and a couscous and almond salad; or roasted clams with Manzanilla sherry, couscous and preserved lemon. In the 2005 *Good Food Guide*, launched September 2004, we were named as the favourite Middle Eastern restaurant. It was a thriving hotspot for locals, who'd either grab a reasonably cheap eat or a cocktail or two at the bar while the sun set.

We learnt a lot from this restaurant because it felt like we were always behind the eight ball. Although Moorish was thriving, we didn't realise that soon enough it would become one of the worst business decisions of my life.

20

ALL WITHIN MY HANDS

Before we had opened Lulu and Moorish, Phil Scott, one of the senior guys at Fairfax at the time, gave me a call one day and asked if we could have lunch and talk about a role in the food liftouts that appeared on Tuesdays in the *Sydney Morning Herald* and Melbourne's *The Age*.

Phil basically offered me a position where I'd supply a couple of recipes a week and write a short intro column explaining the theme of the dishes. *Good Living* in Sydney, and *Epicure* in Melbourne were the most read food liftouts in the country, so it was an amazing opportunity to help raise the profile of Salt even more.

But I did have some reservations. I was this young chef in Sydney with a restaurant that was doing really well, and maybe having a weekly food column would piss off a lot of chefs. I was worried people would think my ego was getting too big. Not only that, Fairfax dished up the highest accolades in the industry—chef's hats—in the *Good Food Guide*. At that time Salt had been awarded two chef's hats, three being the highest you can get, so I was also concerned that others might think I was receiving favouritism.

I was so concerned about false perceptions, I told Phil that if I was employed by Fairfax, it was only fair that I hand the chef's hats back. So there I was, bargaining to hand back all that we had worked so hard for, because I was worried what others thought. What a mistake. He said 'don't worry, you don't need to do that, everything will be fine.' He then explained that me doing the recipes would not result in favouritism, and the *Good Food Guide* would never, ever put its integrity in jeopardy.

He was right, and there was never favouritism. Phil further explained that Salt already had two chef's hats awarded and we'd earned them.

There are a lot of inflated egos in this industry, including mine at times. Especially when you are a younger chef looking to make a mark on the industry and you rattle the cage of chefs who had earned their stripes. We all tend to step on each other's toes at one time or another, and looking back now I was as guilty as anyone.

As a result some chefs hated me. Some of them still do. I guess back then it was because I was young, and sure I was a bit cocky too, which didn't help. I'd risen through the ranks quicker than some others to two-hat status and Salt was doing really, really well. I think when that happens all eyes are on you, and people start asking why. They try and find kinks in your armour and you become a marked man.

Anyway, Phil talked me into it and I agreed to a three-year deal. It took up a lot more time than I expected, but for the first year I fell into a pattern and started to enjoy the new responsibility.

LUKE MANGAN

I'd been told there were a number of chefs who had rung Fairfax asking why they had that Mangan idiot doing the food column, and not using them instead?

A few years into the gig, around the time Moorish opened in 2003, one particular column that I wrote put it all in perspective for me.

The column was on British chef Gordon Ramsay. He was beginning to build his empire and was making a name for himself globally, mostly for his food but also for his charismatic use of the 'F' word. What most consumers don't realise is that it's probably the most used word in a chef's vocabulary. Of course, until the whole celebrity chef thing came about, most chefs were kept behind closed doors in the heat of the kitchen where the 'F' word bounced off the walls every service.

I'd met Gordon a few times in London so I knew him to a degree. He was coming out to Australia to promote one of his new cookbooks, so I wrote to him and said 'how about we run a few recipes from your new book and promote it before you come out here?' He was well up for it and said 'yeah no worries, that sounds great.'

It all seemed simple enough to me. I wrote something like 'Gordon's new book will be out soon and it's fantastic, so here's three amazing recipes.' I also wrote 'he'll be out here in two weeks to promote it and I hope to catch up with him and have a cold beer.' Pretty harmless you'd think.

The column came out on a Tuesday morning in both food sections. At that time I lived down at Bondi Beach, and that morning I'd been out for an early morning run and a swim. When I got back home there was a voicemail on my phone from someone I didn't even know. It was a pretty colourful message voicing their opinions about me, my column and things I had written.

'You don't fucking know Gordon, who the fuck do you think you are, you won't be coming out having fucking beers with us, who do you think you are?'

It was madness. It confused the hell out of me.

As much as you like to think it won't affect you, or as much as you say it doesn't, those sort of things do hurt. I'm only human at the end of the day. I rang Lucy and we spoke about it because I really wasn't sure how to deal with it. She was very supportive, as she always was, and she said not to let it bother me, just forget about it and get on with it.

Unfortunately though, I got hot under the collar and rang back and left a message myself. It was a stupid thing to do. I should have just hung up. I basically did exactly the same thing. It was a really childish, hot-headed response and I really regret doing it. Perhaps that person regrets it too. But I guess I'll never know because that was that. It was then that I started to get paranoid about the impact the column was having on people's perception of me.

When I look back now it all seems so stupid, but I was young and sometimes it worried me what people thought and said about me. I was already aware that there was a lot of jealousy floating around too. It suddenly didn't seem worth it.

I decided to rid myself of all that stupid crap and when my contract came up for the column I decided not to renew it, especially as I had just been offered a full-time role as the *Today Show* chef on Channel Nine. I loved doing the column but it felt like I was travelling down a dirty road that I didn't want to go down. Now though, with the benefit of hindsight, if an offer like that came my way again I wouldn't give a fuck. I'd do it. In fact I'd probably deliberately write things to wind people up even more, because I'm stronger now.

What I realised out of that whole mess was that sometimes, no matter what you do, it's gonna piss off someone. And the reality is you have to pick your fights carefully. There will always be someone there to take a swing. It made me realise that all I need to do is concentrate on what I do, and make sure I do it well. That's all that matters. There will always be knockers, but it's important to always remember there will always be people who like what you do too. And I can't control any of that. All I can control is what I do.

Salt was doing really well, so I just decided to knuckle down. That's really when I started to build the brand and become more focused on, and driven about, my own goals. It was all within my hands.

21

IN BED WITH VIRGIN

Guests often ask if they can see the chef. More often than not it's just to praise you for a wonderful dinner. Sometimes it's to complain about their evening, or because they're regulars and would love to say g'day. On the odd occasion it's a businessperson with a sudden idea that could include you, but most of it is wine-fuelled bravado and little comes of it.

One night at Salt, four guys were sitting on table 2 near the kitchen. I was on the pass and they were watching our every move. It's nothing new, especially for an open kitchen. I prefer open kitchens, I think they deliver a sense of theatre. The chefs can see the guests and understand where they are at with their evening, and diners can see the kitchen at work preparing their dinner.

So here we were in the middle of service: pans were clanging, dishes were hitting the pass, getting my approval and then being whisked away by waitstaff to please the room full of punters.

One of the gentlemen on this table of four sitting near the kitchen grabbed the attention of a waiter to tell me they'd had a great meal and wanted a quick chat. I said 'no problem, let them know that once the kitchen cools down a bit I'll be over.'

When the heat is off in the kitchen and everything has settled down and in control, I think it's important for the chef to come out and say hi to guests, especially if it's their own business. Sure you get flattery, but it's also great advertising for the restaurant, and it can also help you understand anything that you can change. Guests are often very matter-of-fact about their experience.

I ducked out of the kitchen to say a quick hello. They explained that they were out from England and their boss was coming out in a month's time. They'd love him to come and eat here.

Keep in mind this kind of thing happens in restaurants. The amount of business cards, promises, possible meet and greets are endless, so at the time I didn't think much of it. I said 'no problem, here's my card, tell your boss to give me a call and we'll look after him.'

Then I asked 'By the way what do you guys do?'

They all responded almost simultaneously 'we work for Virgin.'

Sometimes it takes me a while to put two and two together, and without thinking I stupidly asked 'so who's your boss then?'

They looked at each other and then one of them replied 'Sir Richard Branson.'

I nearly fell off my chair.

It was a bit of a thrill, I just remember when they left I thought, *how cool would it be to have Richard Branson eat here.* I had a laugh with my staff about it, and then I really didn't think about it after that evening.

About a month later we were setting up for the busy Friday double. It must have been just on midday because we were about to open the doors at Salt. I was in the kitchen talking to my chefs when my mobile rang. I answered it and this guy with an English accent said 'Hi Luke, this is Richard Branson.'

I was thinking, *yeah, right, someone is taking the piss here.* All my staff knew about the evening a month back, and surely one of them was playing a prank on me.

So I sussed him out and played along. 'Oh yeah, how can I help?' I said.

'A couple of my managers were in at your restaurant a month ago and said I have got to come and see what you're doing.'

It dawned on me: this actually was Richard Branson.

'Can we come in for lunch today?' he asked.

We were completely booked at Salt. So I asked 'how many people?'

'Ten people at about 12:30pm?' he replied.

Fuck. A table for ten people on a Friday lunch and the doors were about to open. We couldn't move people or even squish tables together. Salt was booked solid. I couldn't fit him in. We had Moorish at the time, so I said 'Well we can't fit you in here at Salt. Why don't you go to the Bondi restaurant and you can enjoy beautiful Bondi Beach and have a great lunch?'

'That sounds lovely,' he said.

Strewth, ten people for lunch on a Friday with this much notice, and on top of it it's Sir Richard Branson and nine other people that could be from anywhere. They could be actors, his employees, musicians, friends?

He then said 'will you be there? I'd love to meet you.'

I was standing there in my whites in the kitchen at Salt, just before we opened for service. But my immediate response was 'yeah sure okay, I'll come down and meet you, no problem.'

I rang Moorish immediately and got them to find a space for ten people. I had a quick word with my head chef Mark and then I rushed down there.

I'm not sure why I was so intent on meeting him and sorting it out. Perhaps in the back of my mind I thought there was a fair chance the media and paparazzi would be down there, and it might be a great opportunity to advertise the business. And although I've always believed that you treat everyone the same in your restaurant, that everyone's money is the same colour, opportunities through positive media are moments not to be missed.

We were chockablock full for lunch at Moorish as well, but it was a much bigger restaurant than Salt, so we moved a few things around quickly and arranged a table of ten on the balcony overlooking Bondi Beach.

Sure enough, in comes Richard, and some other people from Virgin music including Deni Hines.

I ordered a couple of bottles of champagne for the table, and he asked me to come and join them for a glass. I remember sitting there thinking, *what the hell is happening today? This is madness.*

He was a really nice, interesting guy and we had a pleasant chat but I had to get back to Salt. I excused myself, thanked him and his guests for coming to my restaurant and headed back.

And that was that, or so I thought.

That night I was busy in the throes of service at Salt when my mobile rang. It was Richard Branson.

I froze for a moment. My heart skipped a beat, then it pounded against my chest. Oh fuck, maybe they had a bad experience, or worse, someone got food poisoning. It'd make global news. 'Richard Branson poisoned by Aussie chef.'

He said 'Hi Luke, I want to bring my wife Joan into your restaurant Salt because she couldn't make lunch today down at Moorish.'

I said 'Yeah, cool, of course, no problem, when would you like to come in for dinner?'

'In about ten minutes,' he replied. 'We are on our way there now.'

I said 'No problem, I'll see you soon.'

Fuck! The restaurant was packed. There were people in the bar on a waiting list to come in, but we pulled in a table from somewhere and made it up in a nice area near the front window. It was panic stations.

He walked in with his wife Joan and everyone in the restaurant literally stopped and watched them. Everyone knew who he was—the staff, the guests—it was amazing, especially for a room that's usually full to the brim with the chatter of jovial people enjoying good food and good company. You could hear people whispering 'hey look, it's Richard Branson.' It was incredible.

I went over and greeted them and he told me he had a lovely lunch, then asked if I could cook for them, just make up a menu. As I mentioned earlier, I enjoy that challenge. When someone just asks you to cook whatever you want you can show off and really dish up a kind of journey through your food.

Towards the end of the evening he asked if I could come over and have a drink and a chat at his table, and I gladly obliged.

He said 'Luke, I've really enjoyed what you're a doing with your food. We have an airline starting out here in Australia in about eight to ten months' time for Virgin Atlantic, we'd love you to do the food on it.'

'Are you serious?' I asked.

'Of course,' he replied.

I was in shock, but it wasn't the first time I'd been approached for a consulting chef gig for an airline. In 2000 British Airways had contacted me about doing their food, particularly the England to Australia route.

We had arranged a breakfast meeting at Salt one Saturday to discuss the project and whether it would work for both parties. I arranged a bunch of pastries and coffee for everyone, we sat down, then I presented a printed menu of ideas that I thought would work on their airline.

It was a pretty short-lived meeting. British Airways weren't there to read a piece of paper, they were expecting me to present all the dishes: a full tasting of a proposed menu that I thought would work for their clientele. I gave them a piece of paper with ideas scribbled on it with coffee and croissants! What an idiot.

I wasn't the only chef being considered either. From what I heard after my debacle of a meeting, all the other chefs prepared full tastings. I felt like a complete muppet. That was a major mistake because I didn't understand what I was getting myself into. I wasn't prepared properly for that meeting and I guess I hadn't really read emails properly.

To be honest at that time in my life I was pretty shot. I was all over the place really. Lucy and I were going through the break-up all while trying to control the reigns of Salt, which was seriously busy. I probably wasn't thinking straight. I just didn't give it the attention and respect it required.

Liam Tomlin, a wonderful chef and most known for Banc, ended up getting the British Airways gig. I knew Liam really well then, we were pretty close, so I asked him what he did when he saw British Airways management. He told me they came in and he cooked all this food for them to try, then they discussed what would work and how things could change if they needed to.

I realised I was a complete fucking idiot. Coffee and croissants? What was I thinking?

It was something I fucked up on, big time. But I learned from the British Airways meeting. That was a huge opportunity I had let slip through my hands. Sure there's every chance in the world I might not have been considered even if I had prepared a full tasting. Pretty stupid not to give the opportunity 150 per cent though. I decided that if an offer like that was to come my way again I needed to be more proactive about it, follow it up and give it my full attention.

This time, with arguably the world's finest entrepreneur Sir Richard Branson sitting directly next to me, I was all ears, especially because his book *Losing My Virginity* was the only book I'd fully read in my life.

He then said to me 'look, think about it, but in the meantime I have an island in the Caribbean. I'd love you to come out and cook a few dinners for some people.'

Was I dreaming? This was insane. Chef for Virgin Atlantic? Cooking for guests on a private island? Immediately I said 'yeah, that would be fantastic.'

After a few weeks I got a phone call from Jon Brown, who runs Richard's hotel division. He told me that Richard wanted me to fly over to Necker Island in the British Virgin Islands to cook for him and some friends in September.

I got pretty nervous. I had no idea if they wanted dinners for 300 people. I asked 'how many people will we be cooking for, and what will we be cooking?'

He said 'there will be a few dinners, maybe about 15 to 20 people.'

I said to him 'well I'm going to need to bring some chefs.'

He said 'no problem what do you want?'

I said 'three chefs and myself', and I asked if I could bring my girlfriend at the time, Nicola Duguid. I'd met Nicola through Jamie Oliver. She was his PA at the time, but soon enough, upon meeting Richard Branson, that would all change.

So off we went, flying first class to the Caribbean, all expenses taken care of. We arrived on the island only to be whisked away on a speedboat under the late night moonlight. It was like a James Bond film. It was crazy.

It was quite late by the time we arrived at the island. All the staff had waited for our arrival and were waving from the shoreline as we approached. Then they laid on a late-night feast for us as well.

We all had our own rooms and there was a little note on my bed from Richard saying 'Welcome to Necker Island. I hope you enjoy it here and I'd love to have breakfast with you in the morning.'

I woke the next morning and the view from my room was crystal clear ocean as far as the eye could see: kilometres of blue until it shimmered into the horizon.

Necker Island is incredible. Richard has about 18 rooms on the island, and it's a couple of hundred thousand US dollars a week to rent. That's right, a week.

I met Richard and Joan for breakfast at about 8:30am. It was so surreal. During breakfast he said 'look, I really don't need you to do much, there's probably just one dinner I need you to do. I just want you and your team to enjoy the island.'

I was thinking, *okay, um, right, all this way for a dinner?*

We were on the island for 14 days. In the end we did one dinner for some high-profile guests and that was it. The dinner was a breeze.

IN BED WITH VIRGIN

We went out, caught some lobsters and cooked them up. We also took over some Australian salmon, Australian beef and Australian barramundi, and just kept everything nice, simple and fresh.

The rest of the time we went kite-surfing, sailing, windsurfing, waterskiing, kayaking, power-boating and played tennis. I even played a game of tennis against Richard. After the match Richard and I kicked back for a drink and lapped up a bit of sunshine. We talked about Virgin Atlantic, about what he wanted for his upper class clientèle and whether I had the time and interest to be committed to his vision. He was very keen to know what I was doing with my businesses and what my goals and ambitions were. He was also very keen to give me control over the food, as he thought you get the best out of people if you let them do what they do.

I got the gig for Virgin Atlantic. The set-up was a little like a consulting chef role: we presented menus and recipes and gave them to the caterers. They had to make them to our specifications, then we went in and tested the dishes. I'd fly over and check the food out, make sure everything was right and then fly back. It was pretty crazy really.

Strangely, it's not that hard doing airline food. It can get a pretty bad rap, and I've flown economy class on enough airlines to know why. So the chance to do something special with airline food posed an interesting challenge, and I approached it with the same attitude as I do all my food: keep it simple. But that didn't mean a dish could work: there are a few restrictions with heating, size, and preparation time on board. So you might do a nice piece of chicken with braised lentils to keep it moist or a braise where moisture loss might be less of an issue. The thing with airline food is that the whole dish needs to be heated at once, so you need to be mindful of the composition.

LUKE MANGAN

Not long into the Virgin Atlantic gig Nicola and I broke up. We'd lasted about nine or ten months. Richard was back out in Australia at that stage and I had dinner with him at Bistro Lulu. He was looking for a PA, and, sure enough, Nicola ended up being Richard's PA for the next four years. So I'd taken Nicola from Jamie, and I don't think he was too happy as she and Jamie's wife Jools were best of mates, and I'm sure she was Jamie's best PA! Nicola now runs the charity arm of Virgin.

Richard has some resorts around the world, in Morocco, South Africa and of course Necker. We have sent some of my key personnel to do some special dinners on numerous occasions. So I've been doing things for Virgin on and off ever since I met Richard. I became the chef for Virgin America first class, V Australia business class and there are a few other things in the pipeline, so expect to see more of my influence across the Australian domestic part of the airline in the near future.

The only thing left is to do the catering for the Virgin Galactic Spaceship, but perhaps that flight of fancy would be better suited to the molecular gastronomic heights of Heston Blumenthal.

22

DEALT A ROYAL FLUSH

At the beginning of 2004 I received an email from a guy named Matthew Peek. He was the Australian Ambassador to Denmark and in the process of coordinating a celebration week in the lead up to the wedding of Danish Crown Prince Frederick and Australia's Mary Donaldson.

The brief was to promote all that is great about Australia and give the Danes a taste of some of our culture. I'd be a representative of that 'culture' as far as cuisine was concerned. After meeting Princess Mary I was quoted in the *Sydney Morning Herald*, describing her as having some 'natural class' and further explaining that 'she's not one of those Aussie bimbos.' And they asked me to cook for them? Mangan the muppet strikes again! Talk about culture.

No one really ever said why we were chosen to cook as a representative of Australia, but what I do know is that Mary used to come into Salt quite regularly. Before she met Prince Frederick she worked at Bell Property, which was just up the road from Salt in those days. How much has her life changed from being an employee at Bell Property to Princess of Denmark? Amazing. Sure beats winning Employee of the Month.

It was an amazing opportunity. It not only raised my profile abroad, it gave Australians a glimpse of me and how I must be doing something right to get a gig like that. It was such an honour to be seen in that light. The reality is that we all have our interpretations of Australian cuisine, that's the beauty of this country and its chefs. You could have put a hundred Australian chefs in that situation and they would have done the country proud. Our influences are many and our passion is, arguably, second to none.

Who's to say what 'Australian' cuisine is anyway? Neil Perry has a lot of Asian influence, mine has that classic French background, Anthony Musarra has Mediterranean influence, Guy Grossi has a strong Italian background, Tetsuya has Japanese and French influences, and so on. Can it really be defined? For me it's about using great Australian fresh produce and embracing our cultural influences, which I think we all do as Australian chefs.

It was the second week of May 2004 when I took a couple of chefs and flew over to Denmark to cook a series of 'Aussie' dinners. We took stacks of Aussie produce too: about 100 kilograms of Australian lamb, Darrell Lea liquorice, 50 kilograms of Port Lincoln Hiramasa Kingfish… it was brilliant.

We had four or five different dinners to do that week, which were all based loosely around a similar theme, so preparing for each event got easier as the week progressed. We worked in the one-Michelin-star Restaurationen with chef Bo Jacobsen for a couple of nights to promote Australian food, which was a real blast. He's a great chef and a lot of fun, and he welcomed us into his kitchen with open arms. We also did a dinner at the residence of the ambassador.

But the two main gigs were for the royal family and guests. The first was labelled as the Danish Crown Prince's 'bucks' night'. Well, there were women there, as there should be for any bucks', but perhaps not what you're thinking. It wasn't quite what an Aussie might do at a bucks' party, that's for sure. It was a formal royal traditional night for about 150 people, and the Prince Consort and Queen Margrethe were there too. It was full on. We put on a buffet dinner, but Frederick wanted kangaroo included. It's not a very forgiving meat at the best of times, and you have to know what you are doing. It was dangerous, but we pulled it off. We just lightly grilled the 'roo and served it with a chickpea Moroccan dressing, beetroot and feta.

The big one was a special five-course dinner, all matched with Australian wines, for 130 VIPs with Queen Margrethe II, The Prince Consort, Frederick and Marz (as I call her now) at the Frederiksborg Castle, about an hour out of Copenhagen. *60 Minutes* was filming, and were in the kitchen while we are trying to cook this bloody dinner so the pressure was on. The cameras were on the whole time, but we loved it and embraced it. How often does something like this happen? There was press from all over the world in our faces while we were preparing this dinner. At the end of the day we had to ask them to leave because our main objective was to cook this degustation dinner for the VIPs and getting that right was the most important thing.

Frederick and Mary came into the kitchen halfway through service to see me and have a chat about the food. Frederick told me how much he enjoyed one of the dishes and we stood there and talked for about 15 minutes, it was lovely. The kitchen was frantic and, while we were talking, in the back of my mind I was thinking, *is this course going to be ready? Has this chef ensured that the oven is the right temperature?* But what are you going to do? When royalty walks in the room, and you've been hired by them to cook, you're going to be the perfect host!

We nailed it. I was pretty confident and things were going well during the night, and the applause from the guests for my brigade was pretty overwhelming. I'm just pleased that a menu that really sums me up as a chef could have such a positive impact on such important people.

The Danish Royal Menu

Course 1
Coconut broth, Balmain spice and seared scallops

Course 2
Sashimi kingfish with soy ginger shallot dressing, rocket and feta

Course 3
Roast barramundi with lemon and basil scented risotto, sweet pea sauce

Course 4
Lamb loin with mustard crust, asparagus and mustard cress salad

Course 5
Liquorice parfait, lime syrup

Coconut Broth with Balmain Spice and Seared Scallops, Curry Spices

Serves 6

Broth
50g butter
100g eschallots
50g white fish flesh
3 kaffir lime leaves
400ml fish stock
400ml coconut milk
100g coconut milk powder
50g palm sugar
1 kaffir lime leaf, julienne

Garnish
18 sea scallops
15g Sydney spice (from my range of spices)
½ bunch baby coriander, finely chopped
1 sheet nori, chopped into a chiffonade
½ lime, zested

Melt butter in a pot and add eschallots, fish trimmings, lime leaves and cook on a low heat until soft. Add fish stock, coconut milk and powder. Simmer for 10 minutes, then take off the heat and leave the broth to infuse for 20 minutes. Take the lime leaf out, blend and strain through a fine strainer, set aside.

Melt the palm sugar with some water, add the julienne of lime skin and leaf and cook for 2 minutes. Use as part of garnish.

When ready, heat the broth and pan-sear the scallops until just cooked. Place 3 scallops per bowl, sprinkle some of the spice in the bowl and ladle the broth over the top. Garnish with the baby coriander, nori, zest and lime leaf.

Kingfish, Ginger and Eschallots, Fetta and Wild Rocket

Serves 6

Sugar Syrup
150g sugar

Dressing
100g fresh ginger, peeled and sliced
50ml chardonnay vinegar
40g eschallots, peeled and finely diced
10ml soy sauce
100ml extra-virgin olive oil
20ml pickled ginger juice
Sea salt, to taste

600g good quality sashimi kingfish
100g Persian fetta
80g wild rocket, picked

Put sugar and 150ml water in a saucepan and boil until sugar dissolves. Store any leftover syrup in a sterilised jar in the refrigerator for future use.

Peel and slice ginger very thinly with a sharp knife (or mandolin if you have one). Blanch in boiling water 3 times at 2–minute intervals and refresh in cold water each time. Heat sugar syrup and chardonnay vinegar together and pour over blanched ginger and simmer for 3–5 minutes, let it cool. Place in fridge for at least a couple of days, to allow flavours to develop.

Dice pickled ginger as fine as you can, mix with eschallots, soy sauce, olive oil and the juice from the pickled ginger, season.

Slice kingfish thinly with a sharp filleting knife and place flat on a plate, season and coat with ginger and eschallot dressing.

Finish with Persian fetta and wild rocket.

23

YOUNG BLOOD

What has now become known as the Electrolux Appetite for Excellence program began out of my frustration at trying to keep our talented young professionals from leaving the industry. 'Skills shortage' is a term you hear bandied around a hell of a lot. Once you open your own restaurant you soon become disillusioned and depressed at how hard it is to find good apprentices. It's the reason behind my philosophy of keeping staff members who are at the top of their game. If you look after the good ones, they'll stay and deliver on your vision. Shannon, Joe, MJ and Kathy, for instance, have been with me for long periods and are still with me now. You can't buy that kind of loyalty. In this industry it's a bloody rarity.

Once you found an apprentice chef who you thought was up to the task it became an ongoing battle to keep them motivated. There wasn't really much industry-based motivation for them and, as a result, a lot of them were just chucking it in.

Apprentices were getting paid less than 'cooks', who had no formal qualifications. Unqualified chefs were quite often getting paid cash in hand and given sous chef titles, because they were a dab hand at making pizza. It was demoralising for young apprentice chefs. Why bother doing your apprenticeship on bugger all money when you can get a gig in a high-volume food service outlet and get paid practically double for flipping burgers and re-heating sauces? The problem was especially dire down at Moorish, where we would have to ramp up the chefs in the summer. We never employed people without qualifications: it was a principle of mine. It's the grounding you needed to have if you were serious about being a chef, and the sort of chef I wanted in my kitchens had to be serious about their career. Full stop.

We'd place ads week after week after week. You had cooks rolling through the door who'd been working in short-order, high-volume, push-it-out places, so the owners could afford to pay them well. We'd try and hire qualified chefs but we couldn't pay nearly as much.

It was a really difficult situation. You have to remember these guys are young too, they are just starting to party legally, they're all becoming adults and here I am wanting them to work 60-hour weeks and forgo their social life. So it was no surprise that many go for the soft option, and we lost a number of quality apprentices because they just had no motivation. They were as disillusioned as we were. They couldn't see the value in working long hours, doing shit, repetitive jobs in the kitchen for four years. Many of them chose the industry because of the whole glamorous celebrity chef side of things. Apprentices soon came to the harsh realisation that the four years of torture were not going to turn them into Jamie Oliver overnight.

YOUNG BLOOD

I wanted to instil a feeling of opportunity in the younger guys. Lucy and I had been talking about methods to motivate and reward young professionals. It really started off as an idea to do something internally between the three restaurants to try and give a bit of a focus to the younger guys who were working quite hard. In fact, it was an idea that came from a train trip from London to Paris with my good friend Tim Etchells, who started Taste of Sydney festival and was also involved in Jamie Oliver's *Jamie Live*. Tim and I were going to do it together but it never got off the ground.

At the time, Lucy and I were working with Lexus and their fine dining Encore program, where Lexus Encore members could make a booking and we'd keep a table up our sleeve for them at Salt. Our ideas for young chefs came up in conversation over lunch one day, and we weren't too sure how to go about it. Lexus had a very strong food focus within their marketing program. They said, well if you want to do something we'll work it in, and all of a sudden the ball was rolling.

What we didn't realise when we started was how much it was going to cost. It was like starting a new business. Lucy and I sat down and tried to work out how we could make it happen, and how we could pay for it.

We started considering who we had a relationship with, who our corporate partners were. We brainstormed around the companies we were already associated with from our restaurants. We decided to offer Lexus the naming rights. They already loved the idea and were keen to get behind it, so becoming a naming rights sponsor was a no-brainer. We got a few other sponsors behind it, like Sanpellegrino, and in the initial year we even got Sir Richard Branson and Virgin Atlantic involved.

LUKE MANGAN

Lexus paid for naming rights, and in the early days it cost us $250,000 of our own money to make it happen. The program has never made money, which is quite stupid really, but that wasn't our aim. As long as it paid for itself we were happy, because it was something we felt the industry needed. Lexus were absolutely fantastic for the program, from day one up until the day that they were no longer the naming rights sponsor, but we were losing a lot of money. I'd be lying if I said it wasn't a financial burden. My accountant keeps asking me when am I going to stop funding the program, but hopefully it will fund itself soon.

The sole premise of the program was to recognise these great young chefs who were coming up through the ranks and were going to be the next wave to make their mark. I was really worried about getting the support of the industry. When we first started, we only needed a small panel of industry experts. The calibre of industry legends we got on the judging panel that first year was incredible: Tetsuya Wakuda, Guy Grossi, Lyndey Milan, Anthony Musarra and Philip Johnson.

Lyndey was brilliant at making it happen. She was great in initiating it, and giving us access to the kitchens at ACP. She's been very supportive, as have all of the chefs, especially with their time. They don't get paid for the gig, but what they get is inspired young kids filtering through the industry. It's worth more than your weight in gold.

The original line-up are all still on the panel now. And we've expanded five-fold to include professionals from both back and front of house. These include Andrew McConnell, Cath Claringbold, Chris Taylor, David Rayner and Peter Doyle. I get calls from famous chefs wanting to be involved now. That's the level of perception this award now has.

The nice thing is, it isn't about those judges: it's about the industry and giving young kids a chance to go somewhere. Look at the chances I had: going to The Waterside Inn, then getting the help Rowley gave me to step up to another level. Not many people get that sort of opportunity and if the awards can go some way towards achieving that for chefs and waiters it's been worth it.

With sponsors on board, it was all systems go for the inaugural Lexus Young Chef Program. Life was changing for Lucy though. She and her partner, Simon Macdonald, were expecting their first baby, and in March, their daughter Isabelle was born extremely premature. She spent the first 14 weeks of her life in hospital, and eight of those weeks were spent in intensive care. Lucy's life suddenly ground to a halt. She had a very clear perspective on things. The first two weeks of Isabelle's life, Lucy didn't know if she was going to survive, and she suddenly realised there were some very clear decisions that needed to be made.

I remember going to visit Isabelle and Lucy in hospital, and I couldn't believe my eyes. She was so tiny. It was pretty scary seeing her in the incubator, and I remember tears rolling down my cheeks because I thought there was no way she was going to survive. Thankfully she somehow did. She's an amazing little girl and has her mother's qualities: she's a fighter!

It was such an intense time for Lucy, I think she needed something to focus on. I remember her telling me that she could do it from home, or even from the hospital, because she didn't need to be in an office. And she threw her heart and soul into The Young Chef Program. She told me it was a really good distraction from the draining environment in the hospital every day.

Lucy's commitment to the program was integral to its success. To the surprise of both of us, it struck a chord with everyone in the industry experiencing the same problems. It hit a niche that wasn't being filled. It was phenomenal.

The inaugural Young Chef was awarded to Kenneth Bryce from Gianni Vintage Cellar. We had an amazing night and although the guests of honour—Richard Branson and Jamie Oliver—couldn't make the night they both sent video messages for Kenneth that we aired on the night.

Along with the kudos of being Australia's first Lexus Young Chef, Kenneth got the opportunity to do work experience at Jamie Oliver's Fifteen in the UK, and to represent Australia in the Sanpellegrino Cup. The race sees young chefs from different nations cooking a three-course meal in the galley of a yacht while it races around the waterways of Venice. It's the craziest cooking competition in the world, and Kenneth chanced seasickness to do his country proud by coming third. That was only five years ago now, but he has risen through the ranks since to take up the post of head chef at Simpatico Restaurant, Brisbane.

In 2006 Assiette chef Beau Vincent took out the top honours as Lexus Young Chef. I'd managed to secure Mr Michel Roux as the guest of honour. He'd been out to Australia on many occasions, his wife Robyn is in fact a dinkum di Aussie, and as part of his role within the awards Beau had the pleasure of undertaking work experience at The Waterside Inn. Boy was he in for a challenge!

After three successful years it was time to restructure the awards and broaden its appeal. Chefs aren't the only segment of the industry who lack motivation, career paths and incentive: there are waiters too. Their predicament was just as bad as that of the chefs, if not worse. Australia is not like Europe where waiters can embrace and enjoy clear career paths. Lucy knew only too well how hard it was getting in waitstaff who were committed to the business and a career in the industry, so in 2007 we brought in The Young Waiter of the Year to join Young Chef of the Year under the new moniker of 'Appetite for Excellence'.

It proved an immediate success, and young professionals came in droves. We brought a bevy of front of house gurus on board for the judging panel such as Georgia North, Lisa van Haandel, Luke Stringer, Peter Sullivan, Sam Christie, Simon Hill, Tony Bilson and Neil Perry.

The inaugural Lexus Young Waiter went to South Australian Jai Leighton from The Grange Restaurant at Hilton, Adelaide. Meanwhile, South Australia grabbed the quinella with Melanie Gowers from the Adelaide Convention Centre taking out the Lexus Young Chef. They both had the chance to do a stage with the 2008 guest of honour, Mark Edwards, at Nobu London.

In 2008 one of Britain's hottest young chefs, Tom Aikens, came out to Australia as the guest of honour for the awards. Young Chef Jake Nicolson, from Circa, the Prince in Melbourne and Young Waiter Leanne Altmann, from The Manse in Adelaide both beat what was an absolutely stellar line up of young professionals, arguably the best we'd seen. The two got the chance to travel to Europe for work experience in Tom's Kitchen.

It was this year that the Australian media really took us seriously as the bees knees of awards programs, especially for the hospitality industry.

Following the 2008 program, my great friend and public relations guru Judi Hausmann introduced me to John Brown, CEO of Electrolux. Judi, in her indeterminable wisdom, suggested Electrolux take on the mantle of naming rights sponsor for the Awards. John Brown was quick to see the value the program could deliver and was very upfront with the budget they were prepared to put towards it. It was a tough time for every business because the GFC had hit at the time and Lexus weren't selling as many cars as they'd liked and they didn't see the value in it. It was really at a time that Lexus felt they couldn't continue, so we shook hands and he said the best of luck with it. There was no hard feelings at all, sometimes that's the way business is. Since then. Just like Lexus, Electrolux have been brilliant.

It got to a stage were Lucy was practically working on the program full time and it wasn't paying either of us money that was worth the workload. We brought in Phee Gardner, who'd worked with us back in the days of Salt, to take the reigns and ensure the program continued to move forward. It still doesn't make any money but it holds its own.

The Electrolux Appetite for Excellence program kicked off in 2009 and embraced the Young Chef of the Year, Young Waiter of the Year and the new category: Young Restaurateur of the Year, making the perfect trifecta.

Along with this was a major coup obtaining the judging services of Christine Manfield, Peter Gilmore, Lucy Allon and myself for the new award. Not to mention the return of the prodigal 'Thai' son, David Thompson, as the guest of honour. This was a major turning point for the program.

Danielle Gjestland from Wasabi on Noosa became the inaugural Electrolux Young Restaurateur and the awards packed an absolute power punch. Matthew Dempsey from Pettavel Winery Restaurant wowed the judges to be crowned the 2009 Young Chef of the Year, while his state counterpart Alice Heath from Montalto Olive and Wine Grove proved her service skills were second to none with the title of Young Waiter of the Year.

In 2010 Assiette chef Soran Lascelles won the Young Chef title, while Louise Tamayo from Becasse took out top honours as Young

Waiter. On top of this we had our very first joint winners with Young Restaurateur of the Year being awarded to Kim Coronica at Richmond Hill Cafe and Larder, and Thomas Moore from Grazing.

It still surprises me now how important these awards have become in the hospitality calender down under. It's become so large that it now costs over $500,000 a year to run. We've restructured the business so we now have a panel of experts from all sorts of fields to advise us on the best way forward. The board is there to put fresh eyes on the detail that we can get bogged down on sometimes.

I want to take a step back and let it become an industry-driven program rather than a Luke Mangan-driven program, but I will still be heavily involved behind the scenes. Some of the sponsors are on board because of my pull, but I think it's become big enough now to stand on its own two feet.

PART THREE

'A pessimist sees the difficulty in every opportunity; an optimist sees the opportunity in every difficulty.'

Sir Winston Churchill

24

DREAMS DASHED, BUT TOKYO PROMISES

In many ways I'm still a kid at heart: here for a good time, not a long time. In theory that might sound like a lot of fun, but unfortunately it means you do stupid things too.

One evening I was out to dinner with two foodie mates when a bad decision cost me big time.

We'd had a lovely night—great food, lovely wine—but when we left the premises I drove. It was stupid thing to do. I'd obviously had my fill of wine, but thinking I didn't have far to drive, I jumped in the driver's seat and off we went.

My two mates were in the car and we were on our way from the restaurant for a nightcap at my place. We'd hardly even left the restaurant when I turned the corner and ran into the back of a parked car. It was a brand new sports Porsche.

DREAMS DASHED, BUT TOKYO PROMISES

I went for a walk for a bit, and tried to gather my thoughts. Then I thought, *what the hell am I doing walking around, just man up and face the punishment.* So I went to the Paddington Police Station. There was a policemen at the counter with his head down, I said 'Excuse me officer, I ran into a car about 30 minutes ago.'

He looked up at me and said, 'That's you!'

I said 'Umm, yep that's me.'

They were nice guys and I think they knew I had been drinking. They took me for a ride to another police station. I was well over the limit. I ended up blowing 0.16, so I was three times over in fact. What a muppet, I knew I'd be losing my licence, but I had to face court as well. You can't hit someone's car drunk and then drive off and expect to get away with it.

I took my car to a panel beater and asked how much it would cost to fix. A whopping $25,000. Great. Then I had to fix the Porsche. In the end I just forked out for the damage on his car too, and there was $30,000 damage on that. I was $55,000 out of pocket, and it still wasn't over.

We convened at Waverley Court. I had a mate who was a QC, so he got me one of his juniors to represent me. He tried to help but couldn't, it was a dead duck really. I ended up losing my licence for six months.

I'd only just got back from the Princess Mary gig, which had given me a lot of press, and the judge made a few comments about the wedding and someone of my character representing Australia. It was a very embarrassing day. What an idiot. I certainly learned my lesson.

But the crash was just the beginning of what was arguably the worst 12 months of my life.

Moorish had the bones of being a really good restaurant. I guess from the outside looking in it *was* a good restaurant. We were certainly very proud of it. Our commitment to the business meant we had a long list of regulars and the place was always packed to the rafters.

In many ways though, we kind of broke our golden rule for that business by not making sure we had total control. In essence it was really a consultancy gig where we'd run the day-to-day, but it wasn't our vision totally—not like Salt and Lulu. Sure we were hitting the Key Performance Indicators we'd been set, and the business was very busy, but we'd had some disagreements with our partner in Moorish, and decided the best way forward was to resign from our management consultancy. We advised all of our suppliers the day we were exiting, and paid them up until that day. The restaurant closed not long after.

Our lease was up for Lulu within months of our exit at Moorish. We'd opened it on an absolute shoestring. It's not that we didn't have any money, we just didn't want to make a huge investment in the restaurant and we needed the business to work for itself.

If the Lulu situation was different I think we would have kept it. It was a good strong little business. But a rent increase meant that it wasn't viable anymore. We had Lulu for almost five years. And, sadly, it would end up being the last restaurant to go during 2005. It's another restaurant I wish I still had.

Meanwhile, our flagship restaurant Salt had taken a body blow as well.

Salt was an incredible restaurant. It defined me as a chef. We'd held two chef's hats from 2000–2004, but that was all about to change.

I was in Melbourne the night of the *Good Food Guide* launch having dinner with my mate Dickie (Richard Wilkins) at a restaurant in the Crown complex. I was doing a cooking segment on *The Today*

DREAMS DASHED, BUT TOKYO PROMISES

Show out of Melbourne the following morning, so Lucy went along to the awards with a few of our staff.

We were in the middle of dinner when my phone rang. It was Lucy.

'Salt lost a chef's hat,' she said.

'What do you mean?' I asked.

'We've lost a hat, Salt is only one chef's hat. We dropped from 17/20 to 15/20.'

We were both in shock. It was a huge kick in the guts.

The guide only has small reviews in it; it's not like a full pager that you get in *Good Living*. It's just a brief description, and there was no explanation in the review as to why we had had such a monumental drop, and how we lost the chef's hat.

I probably took it a bit too personally at the time. We'd had a string of successful restaurants and it felt like it was tall poppy syndrome: somebody's way of saying 'don't get too cocky'.

Perhaps, deep down, we knew things weren't as they used to be at Salt. We wanted to sign a new lease. The Schwambergs had sold the hotel and we had a new landlord. But we were quite clear about the parameters we would sign this new lease under, and by the time we had come around to signing it the face of dining had changed quite significantly. We'd lost our chef's hat and then the Goods and Services Tax, while it had a very delayed effect on restaurants and we absorbed the costs for so long, was taking its toll. As time went on it got harder and harder to keep up with price rises. Salt grew but the profit margins just got smaller and smaller.

We basically couldn't find a common ground. Lucy and I could both see that the end was inevitable, and we wanted to walk out on the business while we were still happy about it, rather than let it get into the doldrums.

I realised I didn't want to stand in front of the stove any more. Sure I enjoyed it, but after 20 years of cooking I'd had enough of it physically. The business was better served by me looking at it from above.

For the last six months of Salt, Lulu and Moorish, most of my time was spent running between each restaurant and making sure the operational side of things was on track. I had quality chefs in the kitchen who I trusted to handle the food, and that allowed me to step away from the kitchen. I knew for any future business the role that suited me best was to be the restaurateur, while obviously still having an influence over the food we served.

Although the walls were caving in around our businesses, a chance meeting during the last six months of Salt filled the future with promise.

Two Japanese ladies came in for dinner one night at Salt. They asked me to come out and join them at the table for a chat. They started asking me about the business structure, and told me that they'd been to Tetsuya's and Rockpool and thought Salt was the best experience. I thought, *well, that's very nice of them to say that*. Tetsuya's and Rockpool were, and still are, amazing restaurants.

One of the women explained that she was a headhunter for Mitsubishi in Japan, and that she'd love to see this restaurant in a new building that was being built in Tokyo and would be open by 2006.

'Would you be interested?' she asked.

Would I be interested? All my restaurants were turning into dust, of course I was interested.

They flew me over to Japan were I met Port Japan Partners' chief executive Seiki Takahashi, who would eventually become my business partner. He explained his vision and I explained mine. We came to an agreement where he'd buy 50 per cent of the Salt brand for a six-figure sum.

Next stop was to convince Mitsubishi that we had the right plan to move forward.

Going over there and not being able to speak Japanese proved a bit of a hurdle at first, especially when doing a presentation to Mitsubishi. I remember going into the boardroom with Seiki and trying to sell them our concept, but no one spoke English and my Japanese is terrible. I'm pretty sure that my vision got lost in translation, but somehow we managed to win them over.

Salt had its own space, and next to that was another area. They wanted to lease it to someone else, but I said we wanted it. I thought it would make a great wine bar next to the restaurant. To win them over I got them pissed on Australian wine, then I brought out French, Italian and Spanish wines and said 'we want a bar that has wine from all over the world'. They saw the opportunity to showcase the best of all the great wine regions. So World Wine Bar was born: the perfect accompaniment to Salt Tokyo.

I sent my chef Shannon Binnie over to be head chef. The young kid who had walked in off the street with a skateboard under his arm back in the CBD days had matured into a confident chef I knew I could trust. Shannon and I wrote the menu, ensuring it maintained a strong Australian feel through the use of the best produce Australia has to offer.

The restaurant wasn't due to open until 2006 so Seiki came up with a brilliant idea to give Tokyo residents a taste of things to come. We obtained the use of an empty old restaurant site for about eight months and opened a tiny little 20-seat restaurant called Salt Test

Kitchen. This gave Shannon the chance to get used to Japanese culture, and to the suppliers and systems as well. It was a huge success and built a lot of interest in the restaurant, and by the time Salt Tokyo opened Shannon knew what he was doing.

25

HOME BASE

Everything in my life was changing. Salt's time was drawing to a close, and the new lease arrangements just didn't rest easy on us. It was the beginning of the end. The thought of renewing the lease on Bistro Lulu had hit the same sort of snag and that was over too.

I was still consulting to Virgin and we had the Young Chef program up and running, the last business connection with Lucy. On top of that Salt Tokyo was gaining momentum every day. But it wasn't the only thing on my radar.

I'd had a number of discussions with the Hilton group about a possible project within the re-developed Hilton site on George Street in the centre of Sydney. I think they were talking to several chefs for the gig and wanted to make a serious impact on the food scene.

I already had a relationship with the Hilton. I was brought in as a chef consultant on the Auckland Hilton project to get their high-end restaurant White off the ground around 2001. Former US President Bill Clinton was touring Australia and New Zealand at the time and as part of the tour he stayed at the Auckland Hilton.

I had always wanted to meet Bill Clinton. I've always loved what he stood for and the man that he is. As part of his visit I got the opportunity to cook for him, which was pretty amazing, especially being invited to private drinks afterwards. I had the opportunity to meet the man but when I went up to shake his hand I went completely blank. I wanted to say 'hello, it's an honour to meet you' and then try and strike up a conversation. But no, instead I froze and stood there looking like a fucking goldfish, with my mouth open. He must have thought, *this chef is an idiot.*

That Hilton gig gave me the inside running on negotiations on the new restaurant project. For me, the timing couldn't have been better. Salt was coming to an end: I'd sold half the brand and I wasn't going to sign another lease. I focused all my energy into ensuring this deal happened.

Originally they wanted me as a consultant, but I didn't want that. Then it wasn't going to happen because I didn't like the structure: I didn't know if it was for me. The first thing that came to my mind was the state of the old Hilton. It was diabolical and it made me think, *I don't want to be involved with that image.*

Perceptions of hotel restaurants weren't all that great either, and apart from what Serge Dansereau did at the Regent, restaurants in hotels just weren't a cool thing to do. Salt was a bit different because that was in a boutique hotel.

What did it for me was one particular meeting where my opinions were sounded out.

I said 'I don't want to do this if I'm a consultant chef, and I don't want to do it if it's just going to be another hotel restaurant. If I am going to be involved it's going to be a restaurant that I run and you guys have nothing to do with.'

Oded Lifschitz, who at the time was vice president Australasia of Hilton, who's a great guy and instrumental in all of this coming together, looked at me with a wry smile and said 'You're cocky.'

I smiled back and replied 'What, and you're not?' We both laughed, then we did a deal.

In the lead up to the launch of glass brasserie, I went on a fact-finding mission to France to eat, smell, drink and take in some of the finer elements of the great bistros over there.

Joe Pavlovich, who was my head chef at Bistro Lulu and soon to be the head chef of glass brasserie, came along, as did a bloke named Jean-Luc Ferrier, who had worked at Hilton for many years and was the one who got me involved with the Auckland Hilton project.

The three of us went to Nice, Lyon and Paris. Jean-Luc is a great guy and very passionate about the industry. He reminds me of Inspector Closeau from the *Pink Panther* films, especially with his French accent! He was vital in France to break through the language barrier.

For four days all we did was eat and drink: breakfast, lunch and dinner. We'd have a huge breakfast with charcuterie and French croissants, then snacks about an hour and a half later with salamis and pates. After that we'd have a long lunch, then a couple of hours later we'd have afternoon cheeses. Dinner would be epic. We'd be eating duck and foie gras (and heaps of wine, mind you).

One day we went to the market in the morning for breakfast, and then we went to the delicatessen and bought all this cheese and salami and bread, all for the train trip to Paris, which was only two to three hours anyway.

We got on the train and Jean-Luc started cutting up the cheese and dishing up the food, and Joe said 'guys, how much are we going to eat on this trip?' Keep in mind that I'm a small bugger and Jean-Luc is even smaller. Joe, however, is about six foot three and 120 kilograms, you'd think he'd be the last one complaining!

We got to Paris, and immediately went for an afternoon lunch. Because it was our last night on the trip we went out to Dominique Bouchet for a special degustation dinner, all matched with wine. We were sitting there and I looked over at Joe and he was as white as a ghost. I said 'Mate are you okay?'

He said 'yeah I'm okay', but hell he was white a sheet! Joe started to sweat, and all of a sudden he stood up and took off outside to throw up. His body just couldn't take it any more.

Joe came back inside, sat down and said 'I'm not eating any more, I'm sick of food.' Jean-Luc and I couldn't stop laughing. Joe calls it the 'Trip Luke tried to poison me with rich food.'

It was a great trip and we got a great feel for all the nuances that make French food, especially bistro food: the most enjoyable to eat.

We opened glass brasserie in June 2005. Salt had only just closed and any basic products we had left over from Salt came over to the kitchens at glass brasserie.

It was important for Hilton that they didn't want just another hotel restaurant, and it was important to me that glass brasserie wasn't just a hotel restaurant. I wanted a restaurant that just happened to be in a hotel. It's the best thing I could have done, to be honest, and it's just a perfect partnership.

Salt was the foundation to allow me to do everything that I have done since. It put me on the global culinary map and it served as a springboard for everything I do now. glass brasserie has become home. glass brasserie is the restaurant for everyone. It is my foundation for Sydney. If I didn't have glass brasserie, I'm sure I'd be doing something else, but you need a good, reliable base. glass brasserie is the total package.

It is a big restaurant and we need a lot of staff. It's almost like compiling three restaurants into one. We seat 240 here at glass brasserie and if you add up all the seats at Moorish, Lulu and Salt, that's what it was.

The design on the build was already signed off by the time I came into the picture, so in some regards I was a bit nervous. Having been involved with the fitout of CBD and Salt I knew how vital it was to get everything right. When I saw the design—the open kitchen, the high ceilings, the giant mirrors, the wine focus—I just thought, *what more can you ask for? It's perfect.*

I brought in Joe Pavlovich, who was previously my head chef at Bistro Lulu, to run the kitchen. He understood my food philosophy better than anyone: simple food done well with big bold flavours on the plate. He's been amazing for glass brasserie ever since and has a huge influence on the menu there, leading a team of 28 chefs.

So nothing surprised us more than when, in the weekly *Sydney Morning Herald* liftout (*Good Living*), we got one of the worst reviews you could ever read as a restaurant owner. It was written by restaurant critic Matthew Evans who gave glass brasserie a score of 13/20, but to me it read worse than a 13/20.

I was very happy with what our team was delivering to the market and thought a 14, maybe 15, was a more accurate reflection of what we were doing there, but Evans had obviously had a different experience than what I believed we were offering our guests.

LUKE MANGAN

I guess in all honesty 13 is not too bad a score; it's not great, but when I read the actual review it just confused the hell out of me, and I felt like I was under attack. I'd have loved to have more of an explanation of why we were reviewed in this way. Was glass brasserie really that bad?

Truth be known, I was disappointed, especially for my staff. But it turned out to be great for the restaurant.

That night we did 280 people for dinner. It was huge. People could not believe that 'Luke Mangan' was serving this shit, and they wanted to know what it was all about for themselves. People came in with the review in their hands and were sitting there with it open on the table eating the dishes that were listed.

It was fucking incredible, I've never seen anything like it. It totally threw me. We were like, 'wow this is crazy'.

You'd never believe it in a million years, but that bad review was the best thing that ever happened to glass brasserie. I think that if I got a 15/20 people would have thought 'oh it's just another Luke Mangan restaurant, we don't need to check it out, we don't need to see it.'

So thanks, Matthew. Since that review, business has been brilliant and in our first year we had a turnover of $10 million, and is still as consistent as ever.

It does astound me the sort of impact a critic can have on your establishment, both good and bad. I think it's important for young chefs to try and avoid falling into the trap of chasing chef's hats. If the accolades come your way then fair play, it's a reward, or an acknowledgement for your hard work.

Getting that review proved to me that you need to stick to what you believe in and run the business the way you think it should be run. The goal should be to make the business succeed. When you do that, sometimes the accolades just come along anyway.

HOME BASE

In 2007 and 2008 glass brasserie was awarded one chef's hat in the *SMH Good Food Guide*. In 2010 we got a score of 14.5/20. That's just 0.5 off a chef's hat. We must be doing something right.

It's nice to get the media coverage, and it's fair enough that critics have an opinion, but that's all it is: one person's opinion. If I'm up against Guy Grossi in a 100 metre race I might beat him, well I hope I would! But in comparison, who's to say my barramundi dish is better than his barramundi dish? It's opinion rather than fact.

Some restaurants aim to please a critic rather than please their guests. That's a dumb move. More often than not, what the critic wants out of a restaurant is far from the reasons your regulars keep coming back. Who's to say Neil Perry, Tetsuya Wakuda, Armando Percuoco or Luke Mangan is the best chef in Australia? Who's to say Ford makes a better motor car than Holden?

As long as your standards are high and your guests are happy and coming back, then it stands to reason that you should have a successful restaurant.

One thing that I've learned is that having a chef's hat doesn't mean you have a profitable business, but that positive sort of acknowledgement can bring you business.

What's the message here? Don't cook for the media, don't cook for a journalist, cook for yourself and your guests. Young chefs tend to follow trends, and sure I've done that. But soon enough, it falls flat on its face. Really, you need to be true to yourself. That's all that matters.

From day dot at glass brasserie, and for each project since, my role has changed from what it was in the era of CBD and Salt. I don't want to be physically in the kitchen everyday. Do I want to go through yelling at staff again and putting myself through the pressure? Not a chance. My businesses are best served by me taking a step back and controlling things from above. I get the right chef in there to lead the team, between us we create the menus and I monitor the direction of the business. At glass brasserie alone we have about 80 staff. I've got wonderful staff, but that's 80 potential problems. You can't be cooped up in the kitchen with your head down, your business could turn to custard.

Along with being such a big business, comes all sorts of unwanted attention too.

Joe came to me one day at glass brasserie and said, 'I don't know how to tell you but this guy has offered me cash so we use his product.'

I've been approached on numerous occasions by a person with a brown envelope of cash to coax me into using their product. Sure it's only a very small per cent of the market, but it happened back in the early days of CBD and Salt.

I said to Joe, 'Mate you do what you want to do, but the moment you take any cash from any slimeball, they will own you for the rest of your life and somehow they'll get you. You may need the cash more than I do, you do what you think is best, but if it reflects on our business and affects our business then I'll fuck you off. I've been tempted when I had no money. But the reality is you would have to deal with the consequences.'

Joe said 'I am not interested in their money, I don't want to ever do that. I just wanted you to know.'

And he never has. Good lad. I know chefs who have taken the cash, I don't know why they do it.

The key to working with suppliers and distributors is to just look for the best product. If you have to buy meat from four different suppliers, then do it. If you have to buy fish from five different suppliers, then do it. A restaurant like glass brasserie is big business for any one of our suppliers. With such a large turnover, anyone that gets our business will know it's a big account. We have them knocking on our door.

I will go to any butcher, fishmonger or veg supplier and say 'hey if you want our business, we turn over x amount in this restaurant, do me a deal and we'll use your products. Do not offer me cash. I want to see a business arrangement and discounts based on the volume we are buying.'

I've been using Anthony Puharich at Vic's Meats for 15 years. He's a good mate of mine now and we have trust. Any chef should have trust with their supplier. Barry McDonald has supplied me for about 10 years as well. Both are examples of why you need to find the right supplier for what you are trying to achieve.

Look for the best produce, and then look for the best price you can get for it. That's important. If you are paying $10 less per kilo of potatoes and the produce is shit, then what's the point?

26

US ON RADAR, BUT VENTURE HEADS SOUTH

From the first moment I set foot in the United States, particularly New York, I've been fascinated by it. Sure, my first experience saw me bag a boot full of loot in Vegas before indulging myself in some of their best diners, but the USA felt like a special place. I always wanted to do a restaurant in New York. It's the epicentre of everything that is great about the Western world. For many years it was my ultimate dream. I love that city: it embodies everything I love about restaurants, nightlife and the energy of a thriving web of fascinating people. It's an amazing place. If you've never been, you don't know what you're missing out on.

US ON RADAR, BUT VENTURE HEADS SOUTH

After my first experience I made it a sort of mission to go over to the USA every six months and ensure I met the editors of all of the major press and as many successful restaurateurs and chefs as I could, as well as dine in as many venues as possible to try and get a grasp of what makes this incredible food town tick. I met Ruth Reichel, Dana Cowen and a fella who's become a great mate: Drew Nieporent. He's one of America's finest restaurateurs and started Nobu and Nobu London with Nobu Matasuhisa and actor Robert De Niro.

Drew Nieporent is a big thing in America, and he would always take me to events in New York. He'd ring me and say 'what are you doing tonight?' and then we'd be off to something in a flash. One night we went to the launch party of the original *Survivor* TV program, and he introduced me to Tim and Nina Zagat from the *Zagat Guide*, which is New York's equivalent to the *Michelin Guide* and our own *SMH Good Food Guide*. Drew was just brilliant, he'd always introduce me as 'Australia's best chef'. You can't buy that sort of publicity.

In 2003 I flew to New York with Lucy, Shannon Binnie and a couple of others, and prepared an Australian menu for the illustrious James Beard Foundation Dinner: an honour bestowed upon the world's best chefs. To be put in that league was very humbling. The best chefs, restaurateurs and foodies in the USA all attend to see what you are made of. It's an amazing opportunity.

New Yorker and American celebrity chef Jeremiah Tower even came along and wished me luck just an hour before we cooked.

I caught up with Anthony Bourdain that night too. Anthony had been in for dinner at Salt earlier in the year, and now it was his turn to show me his town. The following night we went out for dinner, which was nice, but afterwards we went for a drink to one of the dodgiest bars I'd ever been in. Anthony knew the bikie guy that owned it. It must have been about 2am at this stage and Anthony said 'let's have tequila'. No! Anything but tequila! The barman came out and lined up all these shot glasses for us and we went boom, boom boom. I don't remember a thing after that.

Aussie expat Gordon Elliott played a huge role in my presence in the USA as well. Gordie has always been very supportive of me. He would do things like champion me to the Food Network in America and put me in front of the CEO saying 'this guy is the best chef Australia has ever produced, he should have his own show.' And he still does that sort of thing now. He's a madman, but I love his work.

I don't remember how we met, but I know I met him in the USA. He was doing a show where he'd take a celebrity chef and cook in some stranger's home. The show, *Door Knock Dinners*, appeared on the Food Channel in the USA. He said to me one day 'oh, you'd be great—come and do some episodes.' So I did. It was bloody crazy. The idea of the show was to knock on the door of some random person who had no idea we were arriving, and I had to open their fridge and cook them dinner from whatever is in their kitchen. It was a lot of fun.

In one episode we knocked on the door of a family in Tarrytown, New York. They were a pretty musical family and while I raided their fridge to cook, the family were joined by Kenny 'The Human Orchestra' Mohammed for a bit of a music session. It was a kooky kind of show. I managed to pull together a dish something along the lines of lamb chops with rice, sausages and veal strips topped with mushrooms and a tomato and basil sauce. Crazy stuff.

I met restaurateur and chef Mario Batali through Drew Nieporent. Drew was my New York friend and Mario was getting his name around as the 'real deal'. Mario and I hit it off immediately.

US ON RADAR, BUT VENTURE HEADS SOUTH

The first time we went out was to this little burger place, Pearl Oyster Bar on Cornelia Street around the corner from Mario's restaurant Babbo. He said 'I'll take you to a place that makes the best fish burger you'll ever eat.'

He wasn't wrong, it was fucking fantastic. He still goes there for his fish burger fix twice a month. We were sitting there talking about restaurants and I was telling him I wanted to do a Salt in New York, so he basically sat there and shared all of his knowledge with me on how to go about it New Yorker-style. It was so inspiring.

Sadly, my goal of opening a Salt in New York never transpired, and as things progressed in Australia with other opportunities my burning desire to have a restaurant in New York dwindled. I also came to realise that it was going to be harder than it first seemed. But an opportunity in the USA was just around the corner.

During 2003 I got a call from a lady named Liz O'Connell, who was vice president at Southcorp Wines at the time, to fly to the USA and help launch the '98 Vintage Penfolds Grange. The gig was a tour to release the '98 Grange through a series of dinners in New York, San Francisco and Aspen. How could I pass up that opportunity?

The whole trip was a bit rockstar. I took Shannon and some other chefs with me. We flew first class, and were picked up in limousines. It was insane.

We did the first dinner in New York at Drew Nieporent's restaurant Tribeca Grill, and the room was filled with all the best food and wine writers in the USA.

Although Drew and I were mates, I was mindful to respect his whole kitchen team. It's very important when you go into someone else's kitchen, which we do a lot of now, to go in there with a really good attitude. Chefs have egos as we know, and really you are taking over their kitchen and doing your food in their environment.

While it's not a slap in the face, you have to show respect. I welcome any chef to come in and cook in my kitchen if that scenario happens. In fact we had Brett Graham from The Ledbury in London doing a dinner with the past five Young Chef winners at glass brasserie in August 2010. It was fantastic having great chefs in your kitchen showing what they do.

I always talk to the head chef and say 'we aren't taking over your kitchen, we are here to work together.'

It's important to leave your ego at the door and go in humble. Of course, I had to learn that. The first time I did something like that I went in with my team like an arrogant little twit. We went in and went boom boom boom, did the dinner and left. It was very disrespectful and you soon realise that you don't get the help from the kitchen crew there as a result. If you're interested in their kitchen and their food then both teams come together for the greater good.

We then moved onto Aspen where we cooked for 100 people at the top of a mountain, and then hit San Francisco for the final leg of the trip. The launch was a complete success and Liz O'Connell was rapt.

At the end of 2006 she approached me about a restaurant venture in San Francisco. She wanted to launch an 'Australian' restaurant in San Francisco and thought they had the perfect site for it. Initially I was quite anxious about doing it, but I knew Liz and I trusted her, and I knew she was a very good businesswoman.

It's a big thing to go and do though. There was already a lot on my plate—glass brasserie, Salt Tokyo, Virgin Airlines—and it's a very bold move to step into San Francisco and say 'look, this is Australian food.'

US ON RADAR, BUT VENTURE HEADS SOUTH

The concept was to be small, simple and casual. We had a third partner who was based in America and I didn't really know her, so I wasn't too sure what she was like. I was a bit nervous about having a partnership with people I really didn't know, after all of my experiences to date, so I approached the venture with a bit more caution than I had in the early days.

We went ahead and opened South Food and Wine Bar towards the end of 2007. Straight off the bat we received a pretty good review with 2.5 stars out of four. It also created a bit of publicity for me in the USA. I saw it as a stepping stone to do other things there. I already had somewhat of a regular gig on American TV, and almost every time I went to the USA I was doing morning television.

I sent one of my key chefs over to run the kitchen as head chef, but for one reason or another she didn't work out for us. I found a local guy to man the pans and keep things at the level we wanted.

For two and a half years it moved along nicely and turned over a small profit. Then the dreaded GFC kicked in. Overnight the business was cut in half. It was incredible. The punters just literally stopped coming in, and panic really set in over there.

We had to look at ways of cutting costs. It was a pretty small place, and when you don't have a lot of seats in a restaurant it makes it tougher to make a profit. Bums on seats is the key to any restaurant's survival. I wish we'd opened a bigger place because I think we could have done a higher turnover.

In the end Liz and I ended up selling our shares and our other partner has taken it on a different direction. It's a French bistro now called Marlowe.

I was glad to be rid of it, to be honest. A bit of money was lost on South Food and Wine Bar and in the pursuit of South LA, which thankfully never happened.

The GFC had a monumental impact on the US restaurant industry. It was tough in most countries. You can't control an economic downturn like that, but as a business you have to deal with it and make sure you have the systems in place to adapt and pull through it.

When the GFC hit hard in 2009, the thing that was important to me was that we weren't going to change our product. I didn't want to compromise on the quality of the beef we use, or the fish we use. The only thing we could do was cut the staff, because pretty much all your other costs are set.

We didn't have to do that at glass brasserie; in fact, we didn't change anything we did in Australia. The ramifications in Australia were much smaller than other countries. If anything, our lunches were down, but at night the restaurant was still pumping.

Meanwhile, at Salt Tokyo we didn't change the format, but we have World Wine Bar attached. It was interesting because where we lost business in the main restaurant, we gained massively in the wine bar. It offered more casual eating, and we ended up being 120 per cent up on turnover in the bar as a result.

Consumers weren't changing their habits: what they changed was their average spend. They'd still want to go out somewhere but perhaps spend $60 instead of $120.

We made a smart decision to get some pastas on the menu and change the concept for a short period to get the bums on seats without disbanding our core operation. It worked a treat.

27

GETTING MY SEA LEGS

In 2008 we held the Appetite for Excellence Awards ceremony in a funky warehouse in Alexandria. British chef Tom Aikens was our guest of honour and as part of the prize the young chef and young waiter of the year received a stage at his restaurant Tom's Kitchen.

The evening was winding down and everyone was starting to leave. Since all my formal obligations were over I joined my mates in the industry to revel in the success of all the young talent Australia has on offer. I'd had quite a few drinks by this stage and was feeling fairly jovial when this really nice guy came up, introduced himself and said 'thanks Luke, I had a really nice night.'

I had no idea who he was, so I asked him 'what do you do?'

It was Sture Myrmell, vice president of hotel operations, Carnival Australia. Carnival is a pretty large corporation, representing a huge group of international cruise liners in Australia including P&O Cruises, Cunard, Princess Cruises, Costa Cruises and Seabourn.

I was a little bit pissed, and being a bit cheeky I said to him 'we should do a restaurant together on one of your ships sometime.' He looked at me a bit funny, and then we wished each other a good night and off he went. It's the sort of banter most people engage in at a social gathering, and really it's just chit-chat and back-slapping half the time.

About three months later I got a phone call from a guy who said 'Hi Luke, I don't know if you remember me. It's Sture Myrmell, I met you at the Young Chef Awards earlier this year, I'm from Carnival Australia.'

I had no idea who he was at first. I couldn't remember anything, so I said 'Umm yeah, sort of, but go on.'

He said 'You proposed the idea of doing a restaurant on one of our ships, would you still fancy doing that?'

Then it dawned on me and I remembered making that comment, and so I said 'how about we meet up and have a coffee and talk about it?'

He came into glass brasserie and we had lunch to discuss what he had in mind. He was a lovely guy and we had a great meeting, and he said they had all these ideas for P&O, which included me and my brand on their ships.

I was very tentative at the idea of putting a restaurant on a cruise ship. I was working very hard on my brand and the thought of branding my company to be a cruise ship restaurant... let's face it, cruise ships, well, they've had a bad reputation in many instances.

To their credit, P&O were looking to address all of these negative perceptions, and that's where I came in. He told me about this grand plan to change the view of the P&O brand, and that me having a Salt grill by Luke Mangan on P&O was one step of many steps in that initiative. They wanted people to know they were taking it seriously. But I walked away from that meeting thinking, *I don't want to be associated with P&O*, it just didn't feel right.

It took me back to the meeting I had with Hilton five or six years prior, where they said 'we have a whole new hotel, we are going to change it'. I thought initially *I don't want to be involved with Hilton*, and we all know what the old Hilton looked like. But look at the change they've made: it's incredible.

I decided to have a think about it.

If you have two parties wanting the same thing it can work. If P&O wanted Buffet Food by Luke Mangan when I wanted to do a proper a la carte restaurant, then it just wasn't going to work. As I had said to Hilton, the restaurant and kitchen has to be completely separate to the Hilton Hotel. I wanted it to be a standalone restaurant that just happened to be in a hotel.

I did the same to P&O. I said 'if you want us to do it, then it needs to be totally separate from every other food and beverage operation on the ship. A separate kitchen and a proper restaurant.'

Their response was simple and to the point. 'We'll do what we have to do to make it happen.'

For any business deal to work you have to remember it's a partnership. You have to be fair and meet in the middle. You have to understand and learn to compromise.

Salt grill by Luke Mangan was born and first appeared on *Pacific Jewel* in 2009. Basically it's a licensing deal and a good part of our business set-up. The licensing deal means I own the brand Salt grill. I sold 50 per cent of the brand 'Salt' to the Japanese company, but I own Salt grill by Luke Mangan.

LUKE MANGAN

It simply boils down to: they have bought my name. We could have called the restaurant anything really: 'Floating Treasure by Luke Mangan', or perhaps 'Not Another Restaurant by Luke Mangan', which might please some people. The Salt grill name worked with the fact that it was on the sea.

When we launched the ship, Joe Pavlovich and I went on board for the first month and made sure everything was in order. Life on a cruise ship is certainly, well, interesting. There's no escape, but to be fair when you open a new restaurant on land there's no escape either. When we opened glass brasserie I lived in the Hilton Hotel upstairs for nearly three months. You have to live and breathe it the first few months to make sure everything is in order.

Salt grill by Luke Mangan is essentially a modern Australian grill. Starters, meats from the grill, fish from the grill; simple food but full of flavour and attention to detail.

Anyone can come to the restaurant while on board the ship, though passengers are required to pay a surcharge to eat at Salt grill by Luke Mangan. It's all about great Australian beef, Australian seafood and a wine list that is totally Australian.

Our second restaurant opened in May 2010 on the *Pacific Dawn* and the design is one of the best I've seen. That means a lot if you compare it to glass brasserie in Sydney Hilton, as that design is pretty amazing, too, in my opinion.

The chefs work three months on then one month off, so staffing can be a nightmare at times. None of the staff I have would work like that, so we had to select a bunch of senior chefs from across the cruise industry and brought them into glass brasserie and Salt Tokyo to train them.

We have our own cool rooms and there's a butcher and a fishmonger. Every time we stop at a port we get in new fresh produce.

Thank God it's worked. It's done so well, in fact, that following the initial launch on the *Pacific Jewel*, we opened a second on the *Pacific Dawn* and another on the *Pacific Pearl*.

Working with Sture and Lars Kristiansen, director of food and beverage operations for Carnival Australia, has been amazing. They both have incredible passion and vision, and because of that we have had a fantastic partnership.

Who would have thought it? It's not something I had ever imagined in my wildest dreams, but life throws up some pretty weird challenges.

28

THESE DAYS

In essence I'm a restaurateur with my hands in many cookie jars. Although our approach towards new restaurant ventures is all about risk minimisation, and each deal is carefully considered in accordance with our brand perception, on a personal level a part of what I'm doing is taking myself out of my comfort zone to try new and exciting mediums.

I made an eight-episode series called *Appetizing Adventures with Luke Mangan*, which screened in the USA and Asia in 2008. The series took three months to pull together. Filming TV shows is certainly not what you think it is. Often it's sunrise to midnight for days on end to get the right footage that all gets squeezed into a half-hour episode. I was used to doing live television where you'd turn up, cook, clean down and leave. It was easy. So *Appetizing*

THESE DAYS

Adventures was a real challenge, especially fitting it into my regular schedule.

The concept of the show revolves around me going to a city, meeting some of the local food producers and local chefs then coming back to glass brasserie to cook up a feast inspired by my travels. I'd sit down at the table with a group of friends and we'd discuss whether it worked or not.

We picked a different country for each episode, and the series included Vietnam, Thailand, India, Korea, Japan, Singapore, Hong Kong, the Philippines and of course Sydney for each finale.

Here I was, the kid with an Irish-Australian upbringing with a fear of spicy food, doing an eight-series show trying the delicacies of Asia. What was I thinking? My fear wasn't limited to the thought of spice though, I was scared of eating dodgy food too. Sometimes you just have no idea what you are eating in the hawker markets of Asia.

In a local market in Ho Chi Minh City, Vietnam I was talked into consuming a traditional drink by a gamut of locals. It had alcohol with snake's blood in it. Although I have a keen sense of adventure, when it comes to food I'm certainly no Anthony Bourdain. But not wanting to offend everyone I poured it into my mouth. It was fucking terrible. I spat it out everywhere and all the locals gut-laughed at me. It was pretty funny, they knew I couldn't hack it!

The water markets in Vietnam were a real eye opener. We would weave through the boats and pick the produce that we wanted, throw it on our boat then hoon off to cook it up.

When we were filming in Singapore, my last meal was at the Hawker Markets and I ate with a lovely local family. The family made a traditional chilli mudcrab and I joined them at their house for the meal. Boy, it was damn hot. I was sitting there sweating as usual, really struggling with the heat. Then the grandmother picked up a scud chilli and ate it whole, and laughed at me. I just thought, *my god the woman is obviously mad*. Scarily, it didn't even bother her. Then one of the kids had one, and his face went bright red, but he seemed to handle it. Then, my worst fear, they tried to get me to eat one, but they had no chance!

I thought all my nightmares would come true in Mumbai, India. The Indians are renowned for some pretty bloody spicy food so I was expecting a torrid time. To my surprise, and my relief, there was more fragrant spice than heat spice. The way they use cinnamon and cloves, it was just beautiful. I loved India.

The intention was to make another series and air it in Australia as well but to be honest I didn't have the time to take away from the restaurants for another three to four months in one hit. Of course, if something good comes along and I can manage it with the balance of the restaurants, then who knows!

More recently we filmed a couple of pilots for a show called *Food for Thought*. It's a bit different to touring the hawker markets of Asia. For a change it's a show where I'm not cooking—I'm hosting. It's like a talk show for foodies. Think Denton or Parkinson, only I'm the muppet asking the questions instead.

My guests are always famous foodies like Stephanie Alexander, Maggie Beer, Guy Grossi, Tony Bilson, Neil Perry or even Tetsuya Wakuda. I interview them in front of a live audience and talk about how they started, what they do, and their cooking philosophy, and then at the end we get up and cook a dish together. It's a lot of fun and lets the audience see the person behind the food.

On the first two episodes we put together, I interviewed Guy Grossi and Tony Bilson. Fingers crossed, we'll get the green light to do a whole series.

THESE DAYS

I guess when you get on a roll opportunities come knocking.

Melbourne was still my hometown and yet I'd never had my own restaurant there. My mate Chris Lynch knew some guys who owned some pubs in Melbourne, so I met up with them. That is how The Palace came about. My partners there are a good bunch of guys and own eight or nine pubs in Melbourne. They're real publicans. I went down and met Mick and Nick. So the deal was done, and I knew it was the right time because the GFC had hit and the food I wanted to do there was really casual.

I'm a bit more mature these days than perhaps the days of Moorish. I thought about The Palace project, considered the pluses and minuses and eventually came to the conclusion that it posed a great opportunity to give my hometown an offering of the food I love: simple bistro grub.

My man MJ, who has been cheffing for me and Joe since 2004 at Bistro Lulu, is on the ground as our head chef. He has really done us proud. It's simple heart-warming food, like Kingfish carpaccio with goat's feta, rocket, ginger eschalot dressing, wild mushroom chervil risotto and shaved Parmesan, braised lamb shanks with celeriac mash, baby vegetables, Madeira jus, or a simple steak from the grill with green beans and bernaise sauce.

When you are building a brand and a profile it's important not to latch onto every offer that comes your way. Deals came my way, like a few frozen food promotions that I decided not to endorse, and I'm glad I didn't. I remember one time there was a frozen TV dinner, not just frozen food. You know, ten grand to do an advertisement for something like frozen food is a big carrot, which I probably could have done with at the time. But you learn to realise what is the right thing to do for your brand.

LUKE MANGAN

I'm not knocking other chefs for promoting whatever they want to. In the end everyone creates their own paths.

Because we were doing so much overseas, I wanted to take some of the best Australian produce over there. Starting all the Luke Mangan brands really emanated from that: promoting quality ingredients, and making sure people knew they were Australian. Whenever I've been promoted overseas, cooking on TV or in the press it's always been about Australian produce and Australian food.

We now have a range of Luke Mangan olive oils, spices, and wines. It's amazing to think there are such great products out there, and that I'm fortunate enough to have my name on them. I blended my first wine in 2010: a Tarrawarra Chardonnay and a Tarrawarra Pinot. That's what I'm going to start doing more and more. People might say 'what do you know about wines?' But to me it's all personal taste and I had a ball blending the wines. I learnt a lot from it.

Salt was great and it gave me the base to create a business model, but for where I wanted to be—basically not being tied to a kitchen for the rest of my life—selling half of Salt to my Japanese partner was the best thing I could have done.

Funny thing is, we looked at doing Salt and Lulu under the one roof. The idea was to have a 30–40 seat Salt out the back and big Lulu bistro out the front. Salt was going to have a private entrance, but they'd run out of the same huge site. In the end it just never happened. Maybe the idea will come around again and perhaps it'll be my retirement venture.

But Salt grill is where I'm focusing my attention as we move forward. We are looking to take it to the world. We just opened Salt grill Singapore, on the 55th floor of the ION building. Salt grill, for me, is about taking the simple version of Salt, and the wonderful thing about Australian cuisine, to the world.

We've got a wonderful stable of businesses now that all stand alone in their own right: glass brasserie in Sydney, my flagship restaurant, Salt Tokyo, The Palace in Melbourne, three Salt grills on P&O, Salt grill Singapore, Salt grill at the new Gold Coast Hilton, Electrolux Appetite for Excellence program and consultancies to Virgin. One of my future goals, pending discussion, is to open a new restaurant in Los Angeles.

As we have grown, it's become evident that I had to expand my business team as well. I already had an agent and PA, but I needed to change the management structure to ensure our business remains consistent and continues to prosper.

In 2010 I brought in a group operations manager, Alasdair France. He worked with us at Lulu all those moons ago and will now deal with all my businesses across the board to ensure we are all on the same page. I've also brought in a business development and communications manager, Mairead O'Connor, because as the brand builds I think the manner in which we represent ourselves can have a major impact on its perception.

I'm very fortunate to have wonderful chefs in the various restaurants. Of course I still have an influence over the food in each of them, but I give each chef a certain degree of autonomy over the balance of the menu. Their self-belief affords me the ability to then focus on the success of all our businesses.

But I don't really know how you judge success. It used to be frustrating when I was in the kitchen at Salt and I would see a waiter taking the meal to the wrong table. Mistakes are something you have to accept as a businessman. You can expand your business as much as you want, but you are still going to have the problems.

So if it was frustrating seeing a simple mistake like taking a dish to the wrong table, imagine what its like trying to juggle so many restaurants without being there for every second. It's about hiring the right management and letting them carry your vision and your standards. They'll never care as much as you, but you can train them to be damn close.

Mistakes happen in all businesses, but as long as you accept that and have procedures in place to try and prevent them, procedures to fix them and the willingness to adapt then you're ahead of 95 per cent of businesses out there.

One thing I know is you don't become successful resting on your laurels. It's about determination and belief in what you do, and mostly it's about hard work and perpetual motion. If you fall off the treadmill, pick yourself up and start running again. Don't give up because you've been knocked down. It's all about getting up on a new day, aiming high, and looking to make the new day a great day.

My work now is about managing my time well and making sure that when people come to dine in any of our restaurants it's the best experience they can get.

I guess if I had to analyse it, I'd say success is waking up in the morning and being able to go and do what you want to do every day, with no compromises!

I'm up around 7am every morning. I have a fresh cup of green sencha tea to wake me up, and then it's straight onto the computer to go through all of my emails.

I get a nightly report from every one of my restaurants, whether it's the cruise ships, Salt Tokyo, The Palace or glass brasserie. These reports detail how many covers we did for lunch, for dinner, what the average spend per head was. It also covers any issues, like if a

THESE DAYS

waiter dropped wine on a guest, if something wasn't cooked properly or, conversely, if we've had some positive praise.

Once I've gone through all of those, I make notes of all the issues I need to address and make all the calls I need to the various chefs and managers. This process is vital to the success of each venue. This process happens every day, without fail.

Some might consider having a handful of restaurants as successful. Having the ability to create opportunities, both for yourself and for the staff that have stuck by you and you have put your faith in, is what it's all about. Watching those staff members blossom by committing themselves to your vision is inspiring. Each and every one of them is an important cog in the wheel of everything I've achieved. To me that's success.

Shannon running Salt Tokyo is what success is all about. He wandered into CBD all those years ago with a skateboard under his arm in search of a job, and now look at the kid. Then there is Joe, who took the reigns at Lulu, and who now runs glass brasserie and assists with all the set-ups in Australia. Joe has a desire to open his own place one day, and he will, but he also understands the ups and downs that will come with your own business!

At the end of the day it always comes back to my passion for food: taking great produce and letting it shine on the plate with a minimum of fuss. If it weren't for the firm grounding I received all those years back—the technique, the application, the knowledge shared, all the blood sweat and tears—then none of this would have been possible.

The commitment of my mentors—Hermann, Michel, Rowley—fuelled the passion in my belly to continually go the extra mile. Once you have that grounding in food, the understanding of the seasons, the produce and the way to balance flavour and nutrition, then the world is your oyster.

The rest is up to you.

What it all boils down to for me is that simple combinations and attention to detail create the perfect dish. I'm at my happiest when I sit down for dinner with my friends and family for a beautiful steak, fries, Bearnaise sauce, green beans and a good red wine. How can you beat that? That's what food is all about, and it's all I've ever wanted to deliver from all of my restaurants.

A successful restaurant is only as good as the passion and commitment of those behind it. Restaurant reviews are not something I really follow nowadays. I know that may sound arrogant, but I learned with my first canning in a review from a knucklehead, that some restaurant critics weren't going to define my business or my life. My customers would define that because they are the ones who keep coming back and make my business a success. Nowadays some chefs would come to me and say 'wow, did you see the bad review on such and such?' I politely say no. In essence I try not to worry what others are doing, or read the reviews. Instead I listen to my customers and worry about how I can continually improve my restaurants.

Don't be fooled either, I am well aware of how important the media are in carrying your message as well. The success of your restaurant can sometimes ride on how the media perceives you. But you know there's nice food journalists out there who really know their stuff.

It's also a matter of being happy and doing what you love. Whether it's cooking for people, running a restaurant, being a high school teacher or fixing cars, it's about doing what you love, and doing the best that you can. If you want it bad enough and you're willing to work hard, I think anyone's dreams can be realised.

I know as well as anyone, everything you've built into the realisations of your dreams can be knocked down and disappear within the blink of an eye if you lose focus for a second.

Even with all my mistakes I'd do it all the same again if I had my time over.

I'm so proud of everything our team has achieved, but mostly I'm looking forward to tomorrow. You just never know what it might bring. Giddy up.

ACKNOWLEDGEMENTS

I dedicate this book to my parents for their commitment. I also hope other parents will take note of the support I was given and understand that cooking is not a 40 hour week job!

I can not thank Michel Roux, Hermann Schneider and Rowley Leigh enough for passing on their passion, John Lepp for his patience and my brother Michael for steering me into this profession and everyone in this amazing industry from suppliers to cooks to the pot washers. What a journey! The produce is the most important thing to me as a cook, and Australia really is the lucky country because we certainly have some of the best produce in the world!

I'd like to thank my good friend and accountant Bob Buckingham from Allan Hall and Partners for helping me through the good times and the bad times and for the fantastic advice along the way.

Thanks to my agents, Michelle Elliott and Jennifer Naughton at RGM.

Belinda Achurch for her support and understanding.

I also thank Anthony Huckstep who has done a brilliant job in putting this book together, all his hard work and long hours have paid off, so thank you mate!

My chefs Shannon Binnie at Salt Tokyo, Joe Pavlovich at glass brasserie, Sydney, MJ at The Palace, Melbourne and Kathy Tindall at Salt grill Singapore, and our partners at Hilton, P&O Cruises, Virgin and my partner in Tokyo Seiki Takahashi and the PJP Group for showing their confidence in me.

Luke Mangan At Home and in the Mood

A collection of some of Luke Mangan's best recipes, emphasising cooking at home, entertaining, barbecuing, simple foods, snacks and food for family and friends.

ISBN: 9781741107302

www.newholland.com.au